Richard Hathaway Edmonds

The South's Redemption

From poverty to prosperity

Richard Hathaway Edmonds

The South's Redemption
From poverty to prosperity

ISBN/EAN: 9783337426538

Printed in Europe, USA, Canada, Australia, Japan

Cover: Foto ©Suzi / pixelio.de

More available books at **www.hansebooks.com**

THE SOUTH'S

REDEMPTION.

FROM POVERTY TO PROSPERITY.

In 1860 the Richest Part of the Country—In 1870 the Poorest—
In 1880 Signs of Improvement—In 1889 Regain-
ing the Position of 1860.

By RICHARD H. EDMONDS.

Editor Manufacturers' Record.

PUBLISHED BY
THE MANUFACTURERS' RECORD CO.
BALTIMORE, MD.
1890.

PRICE 25 CENTS.

A WORD OF EXPLANATION.

With a view to presenting a general summary of the industrial progress of the South from 1880 to 1889, and to give a few facts as to the combination of advantages enjoyed by this section, the matter published in this pamphlet was prepared for the *Manufacturers' Record*, and appeared in that paper on December 21, 1889. The demand for that issue has been so large that it was decided to republish the article in pamphlet form.

R. H. E.

The South's Redemption.

"The South is the coming El Dorado of American adventure. May the Almighty speed and guide her onward progress!" So wrote the Hon. William D. Kelley a few months ago, and every day brings forth new evidence to prove the correctness of his prediction, and to show that without a doubt the South is to be the richest country upon the globe. This is no visionary forecast. Many years will be required to enable the South to attain that position, but not many will have passed before it shall have been demonstrated that this future certainly awaits this section. The combination of advantages possessed by the South for the development of great wealth is not equaled in any other country in Europe or America. In fact, here are combined the chief advantages and resources of nearly all other countries, without their most serious disadvantages.

In climate, soil, mineral and timber wealth, in rivers, large and small, in a long seacoast, in an abundant rainfall, in healthfulness and in every other advantage that could be asked, nature seems to have done her best for this favored land. Every variety of soil, suitable for every branch of agriculture, can be found ready to yield an abundant harvest. The wealth in iron and coal is beyond estimate ; and, in fact, its extent is not yet half known or dreamed of, while no other section possesses such a wide range and such an abundant supply of other minerals needed in the arts and sciences. Of timber there is a seemingly almost unlimited supply, including nearly every variety of hardwoods used for wood-working purposes.

No one can carefully study the remarkable combination of resources which the South enjoys without being convinced that, in natural advantages, this section stands far ahead of any other country in the world ; and with the rapid progress now being made in the development of all these resources, the South is entering upon a period of prosperity greater than any part of this country has ever yet enjoyed. The conditions for this are far more favorable than in the West during the period of the most rapid growth of that region, and this prosperity, being free from fictitious inflation, will be permanent.

At the close of the most disastrous war in the world's history, the South was in a deplorable condition—beyond the power of words to describe. Its business interests had been destroyed; for four years it had been drained of everything that could help to maintain its armies; it had been the battle-ground of millions of men; its cities and its towns were in many places in ruins, its fields devastated and its fences destroyed; blackened chimneys marked the sites where thousands of fine dwellings had stood; its foremost men had been killed by the tens of thousands, and so gloomy was the outlook when the war ended that hundreds of thousands of the young and vigorous men and boys that were growing up left during the next few years for the West and South-west, and for the North; the hundreds of millions of dollars that had been invested in slaves, just as the North invested its earnings in manufactures, were wiped out of existence, though, of course, the slaves themselves remained there; and, added to all these misfortunes, was a disorganized labor system. Then came political misrule and degradation, against which it seemed hopeless to strive. This was only finally overcome scarcely twelve years ago.

It is not extravagant to say that the actual money loss to the South from the war aggregated at least $5,000,000,000. The census of 1870 showed the assessed value of property in the South for that year to be $2,100,000,000 less than in 1860, but this, of course, does not represent the total losses. It does not cover the enormous sums spent in carrying on the war, the loss of so many thousands of the leading men by death and emigration, the chaos resulting from the war, and the disorganized condition of the whole labor system of the country. Taking all these things into consideration, $5,000,000,000 is a very conservative estimate of the South's loss financially.

In 1880 the total amount of capital invested in manufactures in the United States was $2,700,000,000. If we could conceive of some disaster that would have entirely blotted out every manufacturing enterprise in the whole country in 1880, and every dollar invested in them, the aggregate destruction of property would have been only about one-half as great as the losses entailed upon the South by the war. It is impossible to comprehend what it would mean, if at one blow every manufacturing enterprise in this country were wiped out of existence, and yet the sufferings and poverty which would follow such a disaster would hardly be equal to what the South had to face when it laid down its arms in 1865. These facts are mentioned that the South may receive proper credit for the amazing progress which has been made in the last few years.

So rapid has been the industrial advancement of that section during the last eight or nine years, and more especially during the last four, that the business world is now seeking information about every phase of Southern growth, and of the South's resources. Capitalists in Europe and America are looking to the South as the field for investment; manufacturers of iron, cotton and lumber, realizing that the South is destined to control all of these and allied industries, are directing their attention to this section. The cry is no longer "Go West, young man," but "Go South." For the purpose of presenting a general view of what has actually been accomplished in the South, and not simply projected or talked of, this condensed summary has been compiled. Its only aim is to make plain by figures what has been done, and in connection therewith to give a few statements that will carry weight, because they are from the highest authorities, to show what are the possibilities of the South.

In the early part of 1889 many prominent capitalists and manufacturers went South to "spy out the land." Among the number were such men as Hon. Abram S. Hewitt and Hon. Edward Cooper, of the widely-known iron and steel firm of Cooper, Hewitt & Co.; Mr. Andrew Carnegie, the most extensive iron and steel manufacturer in America; Mr. Frederic Taylor, a leading New York banker; Hon. H. B. Peirce, secretary of State of Massachusetts; Hon. D. H. Goodell, governor of New Hampshire, and many others. These are mentioned because of the influence which their statements carry, and because they cannot be charged with being partial to the South.

Letters were written to the *Manufacturers' Record* by a number of these gentlemen, giving their views upon the resources of the South and the progress made by that section in the last few years. Mr. Carnegie wrote that he regarded the South "as Pennsylvania's most formidable industrial enemy in the future."

Mr. Taylor, who made a careful study of the situation in connection with Messrs. Hewitt and Cooper, stated that the South was a revelation to him. "It seemed to me," wrote Mr. Taylor, "that we traveled through a continuous and unbroken strain of what has been aptly termed the music of progress—the whirr of the spindle, the buzz of the saw, the roar of the furnace, and the throb of the locomotive." To the young men of the South he accords high praise for the work which they are doing, and to "the eager, earnest, restless, driving energy which seems to fill them."

Referring to the section through which they passed, he says: "The country through which we traveled was varied, and in many respects beautiful; its valleys fair as the vale of Cashmere, its mountain scenery wild at times as the Alps." "The South, to my mind, is only now on the threshold of its boom." "It has every possible advantage—everything, indeed, that God can give." "The New South has been built up by the indomitable energy and by the hard work of the Southern people themselves," and finally, in closing this most striking letter, Mr. Taylor added, "to any young man, to-day, of pluck and grit with the world before him and his fortune to make, I should say, 'go South, young man, go South.'"

Hon. Henry B. Peirce wrote: "I can add little to what has been so well said, and so many times said, of late, by Northern men who have been South, as to the resources and advantages of that wonderful section which includes Northern Alabama. I am thoroughly convinced that it is to be the great iron center of the world, and that the people will marvel at the growth which will be brought about during the next twenty-five years. The South will receive the greatest direct benefit, because of a revolution socially, politically, industrially and in an educational way, which it will undergo in this process, a revolution so gradual and yet so fraught with immediate blessing that it will be accomplished without friction. I predict for the New South an era of prosperity which shall eclipse any which has ever been achieved in any other section of our great country, so remarkable for its successes in that line."

Sir Lowthian Bell, of England, one of the highest authorities on iron manufacture, recently made the following statement: "Ultimately there seems nothing, so far as our present knowledge permits us to judge, to prevent these Southern States from becoming the cheapest iron-making centers in the Union."

Mr. J. C. Fuller, president of the United States Charcoal Iron Workers' Association, which is composed of all the manufacturers of charcoal iron in the country, while on a visit to the South, said: "I have to-day witnessed what I have hitherto considered existed only in the imagination of the enthusiast. I have seen coal, ore and limestone in almost fabulous deposits in so close proximity to one another as to undoubtedly assure to Alabama the honor of becoming one of the foremost iron-producing regions of the world."

To these strong statements I would add an extract from a letter in the *Manufacturers' Record* by Hon. William D. Kelley, of Pennsylvania, one of the foremost statesmen of the day; a man of broad views, who, though a lover of his own State, looks beyond its borders and sees in the development of the South the future grandeur of this country, and rejoices that whatever builds up this section adds to the prosperity and progress of the United States as one great country. Judge Kelley weighs his words carefully, and hence the following extracts are worthy of thoughtful attention. The most enthusiastic Southerner could not paint a more glowing picture of the South's advantages, the beauty of its scenery, the charm of its climate, the wealth of its mineral resources, and the possibilities of its future.

"In the closing paragraph of my little book, 'The Old South and the New,'" wrote Judge Kelley, "two sentences have caused me much questioning. I say there 'wealth and honor are in the pathway of the New South,' and again, 'she is the coming El Dorado of American adventure.' My friends have thought me too sanguine ; but the States south of the Ohio and east of the Mississippi, with their half million square miles of area, contain a wealth great enough for a continent—a wealth so vast, so varied in its elements and character, so advantageously placed for development, that these States alone can sustain a population far greater than the population of the United States to-day. Their products would be so different from those of other portions of the country as to afford the most profitable exchange, advantageous to all. And it is in these States that we must find the new and greater market for Northern surplus, whether that surplus be in the shape of accumulated labor of the past—that is to say, capital—or the future productions of labor, or of labor itself, because in these Southern States, more than elsewhere, the natural conditions of success exist. As to the rapidity with which it can be done, the past growth of the West furnishes the best answer. It was the building of an empire in the West that relieved and enriched the East as well as the West. The enormous energies, the 'plant' used in that task, unparalleled in the magnitude of the work and the greatness of the reward to all, is now seeking a new field of investment, and there is no spot on earth sufficient for it and within its reach but the South.

"I have traveled much in the South since the war, and have always been keenly interested in every step of progress she has made, and eager to learn all I could of Southern resources and advantages. I have urged my friends to go there, and my son is there now, with all that he has, embarked in a manufacturing enterprise. I do not consider that there ever existed in the West, great as its wealth is, nor in any other portion of the country, anything like the natural wealth of the

South. A very large part of the South is blessed with a climate un-excelled, if equaled, elsewhere in the world. As to the mountainous region of the South, it is richer in natural wealth and in advantages for the development of that wealth; it has a finer climate, better water, and higher condition of health than any region of which I have any knowl-edge, and is, withal, one of the most beautiful regions in the world."

Equally as enthusiastic statements made by other eminent authorities could be given almost without limit. Every honest investigator of the South's advantages freely admits the truth of what has been claimed for that section.

Blessed with such marvellous advantages, what has the South accomplished? is a question which the world has a right to ask. It is needless to enter into any discussion of the reasons why the South did not undergo industrial development prior to the war. Her people pre-ferred to give their attention to agriculture. But it may be well to call attention to the fact that when the census of 1860 was taken the South ranked very high in wealth as compared with the rest of the country, showing that she was not slothful in the business of money-making. In that year the assessed value of property in Georgia was greater than the combined wealth of Maine, New Hampshire, Vermont and Rhode Island. South Carolina was $68,000,000 richer than Rhode Island and New Jersey. Mississippi outranked Connecticut by $160,000,000. In the assessed value of property per capita, Connecticut stood first in rank; Rhode Island, second; South Carolina, third; Mississippi, fourth; Massachusetts, fifth; Louisiana, sixth; Georgia, seventh; District of Columbia, eighth; Florida, ninth; Kentucky, tenth; Alabama, eleventh; Texas, twelfth; New Jersey, thirteenth; Maryland, fourteenth; Arkansas, fifteenth; Virginia, sixteenth, and Ohio, seventeenth. New York and Pennsylvania were also far behind the South in the amount of wealth in proportion to population, the former State ranking twenty-second, and the latter thirtieth. By 1870 there was a startling change. The assessed value of property in New York and Pennsylvania alone was greater than in the whole South; Massachusetts had just one-half as much wealth as the fourteen Southern States combined. South Carolina, which in 1860 had been third in rank in wealth in proportion to the number of her inhabitants, had dropped to be the thirtieth; Georgia, from the seventh to the thirty-ninth; Mississippi, from the fourth place to the thirty-fourth; Alabama, from the eleventh to the forty-fourth; Kentucky, from tenth to twenty-eighth, and the other Southern States had gone down in the same way, while the Northern and Western States had steadily increased in wealth. In 1860 the assessed value of property in South Carolina, according to the census, was $489,000,000, while the combined values in Rhode Island and New Jersey aggregated $421,-000,000, or $68,000,000 less than South Carolina's. In 1870 the combined values in Rhode Island and New Jersey amounted to $868,000,000, and the value in South Carolina was $183,000,000. Thus, while South Carolina had $68,000,000 more assessed property in 1860 than these two States, it had in 1870 $685,000,000 less than they had. In 1860 the total assessed value of property in the United States was $12,000,000,000, and of this the South had $5,200,000,000, or 44 per cent.; in 1870 the total for the country was $14,170,000,000, and of this the South had only $3,064,000,000, or 22 per cent.

The assessed value of property in the South, as already stated, was $2,100,000,000 less in 1870 than in 1860, while in the rest of the country there was an increase of over $4,000,000,000, during that decade. Not until about 1876 were there any decided indications of a change for the better in the South. By 1879-80 an improvement was seen, and it is since that time that the most marked progress has been made. That this progress has been phenomenal, and especially when the poverty of this section at that time is taken into account, the statistics given in this paper will certainly make plain. A comparison of the assessed value of property, by States, in 1880 and 1889, gives the following :

	1880.	1889.	INCREASE.
Maryland	$459,187,408	$477,398,380	$ 18,210,972
Virginia	303,997,613	*344,169,473	40,171,860
North Carolina	169,916,907	217,000,000	47,083,093
South Carolina	129,551,624	145,280,343	15,728,343
Georgia	251,424,651	380,289,314	128,864,663
Florida	31,157,846	93,800,000	62,642,154
Alabama	139,077,328	242,197,531	103,120,203
Mississippi	115,130,651	157,830,431	42,699,780
Louisiana	177,096,459	226,392,288	49,295,827
Texas	311,470,736	710,000,000	398,529,264
Arkansas	91,191,653	166,000,000	74,808,347
Tennessee	211,768,438	325,118,636	113,350,198
West Virginia	146,991,740	183,013,737	36,021,997
Kentucky	375,473,041	551,676,267	176,203,226
Total	$2,913,436,095	$4,220,166,400	$1,306,729,927

*1888.

The census report of 1879-80 estimated that the assessed value of property in the South was only 41 per cent. of the true value. On this basis the true value of property in the South in 1880 was $7,105,917,300, and the value at present $10,293,088,700—a gain of over $3,000,000,000.

The history of many Southern towns during the last five years reads almost like a romance. While Birmingham, Chattanooga, Anniston,

Roanoke, Dallas, Fort Worth and many of the most widely advertised industrial centers have grown with a rapidity that is almost beyond belief, other towns and cities all through the South have kept well up in the march of progress. Louisville, Atlanta, Nashville, Richmond, Charleston, Savannah, Columbus, Knoxville, Memphis, Macon, Augusta, and others, have not fallen much behind the most rapidly growing places. In 1880 Knoxville had 9,000 inhabitants, and the assessed value of its property was $3,485,000; now its population is estimated at 42,000, and the value of its property is $9,500,000. Louisville has increased its population from 123,000 to 227,000, and the capital invested in manufactures from $21,900,000 to $35,000,000. Nashville had a population of 46,000 in 1880, and now has about 110,000. Columbus, Ga., which now has $5,300,000 invested in manufacturing interests, had only $2,400,000 in its manufactures in 1880. Charleston, S. C., which is not much heard of as a manufacturing center, has $7,340,000 invested in manufactures, against $1,824,000 in 1880. Richmond, New Orleans and others of the older cities have made similar progress.

In the newer, or what is known as the booming towns, the gain in population and capital employed in manufacturing has been astonishing. Birmingham and Chattanooga are so well known that it is almost needless to mention their history. Anniston, Ala., which in 1880 had probably 1,200 inhabitants, has now about 12,000. Bessemer, in the same State, which had no existence prior to 1887, now has several million dollars invested in furnaces, rolling mills and kindred enterprises, with 4,000 or 5,000 people living where a forest stood in 1887. Bessemer already has five completed furnaces and two more under construction; and the output of its furnaces during 1890 will, it is expected, be fully 240,000 tons, which is but 50,000 tons less than the whole State of Alabama made in 1887. Sheffield was a cotton field in 1885; its five furnaces alone can now furnish nearly as much freight in tons to the railroads as the cotton crop of the entire South. And to its great pig-iron producing interests it is adding diversified enterprises, such as a $200,000 rolling mill, $200,000 railroad machine shops, and a large number of other enterprises that assure the rapid growth of the place. Roanoke, with its 17,000 people, was Big Lick with 300 inhabitants eight years ago. Heretofore Alabama has led in iron development, but now Virginia is going to enter the race, and new furnaces and other iron enterprises are to be built at Buena Vista, Waynesboro, Salem, Radford, Pulaski, Max Meadows, Graham, Richlands and other points. The whole country tributary to the Norfolk & Western Railroad, which includes the valley of Virginia down to Bristol, Tenn., is moving forward rapidly.

Two years ago Florence, Ala., was one of the most attractive towns in the South as a place of residence; visitors grew enthusiastic over it, and its inhabitants, who numbered about 2,000, thought that no place in America equaled it for attractiveness; but it was simply a beautiful town, and few then looked upon it as destined to be a great city. Its history for eighteen months tells the story of the South's possibilities. A year and a half ago a few energetic Southerners, charmed with it as a place of residence, and realizing its unsurpassed advantages for the manufacture of iron, and the products of iron, cotton and wood, undertook the work of building a manufacturing city. In the short time that has elapsed they have secured the establishment of thirty or more new enterprises, which have an aggregate cash capital of several million dollars. Nearly all are in operation, and the buildings for the rest are under construction. There are two furnaces (one now in blast), a $100,000 wagon factory, a $300,000 hardware factory, and two cotton mills (one in operation and one of 53,000 spindles under construction), and other factories large and small, are to be built at once. These enterprises will employ over 6,000 hands. This has all been done without any real estate speculation; there has been no unhealthy "booming," but simply energetic work on the part of a few people, and from 2,000 its population has increased to probably 10,000 with still more rapid growth in the future now assured. Florence is to be commended for the successful efforts made to secure diversity in its manufactures. In this respect its growth has been remarkable. Instead of centering all attention upon cotton or iron, it has sought to establish a wide range of industries, including almost every line of manufacture from the making of paper-boxes or suspenders to the production of pig iron. This illustrates what the South can do, and is but a sample of what other places are doing and will do in the future.

Less than a year ago Fort Payne was an unknown country village. New Englanders took hold of it, and inside of that brief period have invested several million dollars there in building an industrial town, and now furnaces, large steel works, hardware factory and other plants are under construction. Several thousand busy, progressive people, mainly New Englanders, are vigorously pushing Fort Payne to a leading position among the industrial cities of the South.

Six months ago the name of Middlesborough, Ky., could not have been found upon even the latest railroad maps. It was known to a comparatively few as the place which English capitalists, including many of the foremost iron and steel makers of Great Britain, had selected as the site for building a city on a very broad basis, backed by an apparently unlimited supply of money. Of its advantageous location at Cumberland Gap, where railroads must of necessity meet, and where minerals and timber are in sufficient quantity to supply the most extensive demands of the future, it is needless to speak. Within the last three or four months these facts have been given such wide publicity that they are already well known. Suffice it to say, that for several years these English capitalists had been quietly, but vigorously, at work. Their experts had thoroughly explored the mineral and timber resources of the surrounding country, and over 60,000 acres of picked lands had been purchased. Every arrangement had been made for the establishment of gigantic enterprises before a railroad had reached the place, and before much publicity had been made of their plans regarding the building of a city. Where less than twenty-five people lived half a year ago, there are now, it is estimated, fully 4,000, and Middlesborough is growing as few towns have ever grown. Like Florence, Fort Payne, and other Southern towns that have grown so rapidly, Middlesborough's progress is solid and substantial, founded upon the utilization of the unlimited stores of coal and iron, and the great forests of virgin timber tributary to that place. Over $18,000,000 have already been invested or contracted for investment in the building of railroads, and in the establishment of many and varied industries. Middlesborough is but the visible sign of the faith which the foremost iron and steel makers of England have in the possibilities of cheap iron and steel production in the most favored sections of the South.

Florence, the development of which has been mainly in the hands of Southern men, though Northern capitalists have recently invested over a million dollars there; Fort Payne, "The New England City of the South," which is wholly the work of New England men and money, and Middlesborough, which is the offspring of English capital and brains, but which is now receiving a full measure of American energy and wealth, are three types of the combined forces that are now at work in the South. As such, their progress is of peculiar interest.

THE IRON INTERESTS OF THE SOUTH.

RAPID GROWTH BASED ON SOLID FOUNDATION—THE MANUFACTURE OF BESSEMER IRON AND STEEL.

The growth in the manufacture of iron in the South during the last few years has been so rapid as to attract universal attention. While other industries have made astounding advances, the iron business has commanded the widest attention, and has been more generally discussed than any other industry. This is not surprising, when it is remembered that it was but a few years ago that the iron makers of the North ridiculed, first, the possibility that the South could ever become a large iron producer, and when this fallacy was overthrown, then the idea that the South would become a serious competitor with Pennsylvania in the iron trade of the country was persistently claimed to be absurd.

During the severe depression in the iron business in 1884 and 1885, when many Northern furnaces were compelled to go out of blast, because they could not make iron and sell it at the prices then ruling without a heavy loss, Alabama and Virginia furnaces commenced to invade Eastern markets more freely than ever before. It is of more than passing interest to note that the South's pig iron production attracts the greatest attention during periods of severe depression and low prices. The fact that Southern furnaces continue to run through such periods, and even to make money, while so many Northern furnaces are forced to blow out, is an argument to which there is no reply. The South's percentage of the total production of pig iron is greater during years of dullness than in active times, and this is the best of all tests, for when business is brisk and prices high, nearly all furnaces, even though many may be badly located, can continue in operation. This point was illustrated during the depression of 1884-85. In 1880, the South made 397,301 tons of pig iron; it 1885 it made 712,835 tons—a gain of 315,534 tons. Three States—Virginia, Alabama and Tennessee—which, in 1880, produced 178,006 tons of pig iron, in 1885 produced 552,419 tons—an increase of 374,413 tons, or 139,958 tons more than the net increase in the United States, the production in the whole country outside of these three States being 234,455 tons less in 1885 than in 1880. This condition of affairs was in part repeated during 1888. The extremely low prices then prevailing caused the blowing out of many Northern furnaces, while Southern furnaces were pushed to their utmost capacity, new ones blowing in as fast as completed; and out of the profits made during even the dull times of 1887 and 1888 a number of other furnaces are being built.

In 1884-85, when the shipments of Southern iron to Eastern markets first commenced to attract much attention, but few Northern iron makers believed it possible for Southern furnaces to ship their iron East, paying from $3 to $5 per ton freight, with any profit, and it was repeatedly stated that it was only a question of time how long they could stand what was said to be a heavy loss on every ton thus shipped. Month after month passed by, and Southern furnaces, instead of failing, continued to present every evidence of prosperity, while the men who had had the longest experience in the business, and who it was said must be losing money, went on increasing their production by building new furnaces. This was a phase of the matter which the skeptics could not quite understand, but still they were not fully converted, and various excuses were found to account for the new furnace projects. For a while they credited them to "land speculations," "corner lots," "town booming," and such things, declaring that it was a great bubble which would soon be pricked. About that time, Mr. Samuel Thomas, of the Thomas Iron Company, of Pennsylvania, which is usually supposed to virtually control prices on all Pennsylvania iron, so extensive are its operations, after carefully investigating for himself the resources of Alabama, commenced the erection in that State of one of the finest furnace plants in America. And now, after proving by actual work the profits of iron making there, he is building another furnace and an immense rolling mill, and rumor (which in this case is doubtless correct) says that he will build still other furnaces until his Alabama plant is one of the largest in America. His locating in Alabama was an argument against which the Northern skeptics could bring nothing. The fact that the leading iron maker of Pennsylvania, after close investigation, was willing to back his judgment as to the future of Alabama iron, to the extent of a million dollars, convinced the iron men of the North that it would be folly to attempt to ignore the possibilities of the South in this direction any longer.

The development of the South's iron interests has not been confined simply to the making of pig iron. Not content to make pig iron alone, to be shipped North and there turned into the finished product and re-shipped South in the shape of stoves, agricultural implements, car wheels, iron pipe, and the thousand and one other articles into the manufacture of which pig iron enters, the South is very wisely diversifying its industries by preparing to consume at home the product of its own furnaces, and so great is the progress in this direction that it is already producing almost every variety of goods, from pins and tacks to locomotives. The double freight and the attendant expenses are thus saved, while Southern labor receives the benefit of the work afforded in these varied industries. A large amount of Southern iron will continue to find a market in New York, Pennsylvania and other Eastern States, as well as in the West, and transportation companies will continue to increase their facilities for this business. But while this is true, there will be an ever-increasing home consumption of iron. Rolling mills, pipe works, car wheel and axle works, foundries and machine shops, are multiplying so rapidly that instead of the South being dependent upon other sections for the product of such works, it will soon invade the North and West, not simply with pig iron, but with the finished goods.

According to the United States census report of 1880 on iron and steel manufacture, prepared by Mr. James M. Swank, secretary of the American Iron and Steel Association, and a noted expert, "the average distance over which all the domestic iron ore which is consumed in the blast furnaces of the United States is transported is not less than 400 miles, and the average distance over which the fuel which is used to smelt it is transported is not less than 200 miles. From the ore mines of Lake Superior to the coal of Pennsylvania is one thousand miles. Connellsville coke is taken 600 miles to the blast furnaces of Chicago and 750 miles to the blast furnaces of St. Louis." About one million tons of ore are now annually imported at Baltimore and Philadelphia from Spain, Africa, the Island of Elba and Cuba, and shipped hundreds of miles into the interior to the furnaces of Pennsylvania.

Against this long transportation of ore and fuel to Northern furnaces averaging 400 and 200 miles respectively, with the heavy freight attendant upon it, the furnaces of the South have the advantage of ore, coal and limestone almost at their very doors, and in such close proximity that these three materials can truthfully be said to be side by side. There is no expensive transportation to bring them together at the furnace, for nature has seemingly done her best for this favored territory, as though she intended that here should be the most advantageous point in all the world for the production of pig iron.

In many places in the iron regions of the South the furnaces are literally surrounded by inexhaustible supplies of ore, coal and limestone, the transportation in some cases being but a few hundred yards. This point is enforced in a letter from Mr. R. W. Raymond, a well-known mining engineer, and secretary of the American Institute of Mining Engineers. After investigating the advantages of the Birmingham district, Mr. Raymond wrote :

"Those who had not previously visited the district were impressed with its remarkable advantages for the production of cheap iron. The ore, coking coal and excellent limestone are in contiguity, and it is figured that the total cost of material at furnace in the Birmingham district will average about $1.12½ per ton of iron produced, as against $4 and $5 in the Lehigh and Schuylkill valleys."

Here is an admitted difference of between nearly $3 and $4 a ton, and in many cases the margin is still wider.

As to the cost per ton of iron making in the South, there are so many contingencies to be taken into account that exact figures cannot be given, and the writer prefers not to use Southern estimates, which might be charged with being biased, but to take the testimony of Northern experts. Conservative authorities have put the average as at least $5 less than the average in Pennsylvania. Mr. R. P. Rothwell, C. E. M. E., of New York, editor of the Engineering and Mining Journal, a high authority in metallurgical matters, after a close personal investigation, estimated that the total cost of making iron in certain parts of Alabama, exclusive of interest on capital or profit on mining would be about $8.30, and even this he said had been "bettered," and enough had been done to show that iron could be made there at a figure not exceeding $8 a ton, every expense included. In Mr. Rothwell's estimate he allowed for 1¾ tons of coke at $2 a ton or $3.50 for fuel, but since then it has been demonstrated by actual furnace work that it is possible for one ton of coke to produce a ton of iron, a saving the importance of which can be readily understood, but even if this should not prove possible at all furnaces or on an average, it is undoubtedly true that a considerable reduction can be made from the 1¾-ton estimate.

The Iron Age, the standard Northern authority on iron matters, a year ago, after its editor had spent some time in Alabama, admitted that iron is made there as low as $10.50 to $11 a ton, "including fair allowances for interest on plant, a moderate royalty charge on ore and coal for exhaustion of lands, and a safe margin for ordinary repairs, replacement, taxes and cost of water." "Accepting," says the Age, "the higher figure, and making allowances for freights, commissions and insurance, we find that the furnace men of the Birmingham district can lay down their iron for the average of the grades without suffering any pressure at $15.75 to $16 at New York ; at $16 to $16.50 at New England points and at $15.50 to $16 at Cincinnati. Some of them can do it more cheaply, but at the figures named, with plants run fairly well and producing about 2,000 to 2,200 tons a month, as the majority of them do, the makers in the district would meet the market without suffering. In other words, when standard irons are selling at tidewater at $15.50, $16.50 and $17.50 respectively for gray forge, No. 2 and No. 1, Southern irons could still hold their own." And then, after contrasting some of the advantages of the two sections, the Age closes with the following very strong statement : "But dealing with the industry as it exists to-day, a candid survey of the situation will lead to the admission that if it should come to a struggle between the furnaces in eastern Pennsylvania, New Jersey and New York, which produce chiefly foundry brands for the open market, and the makers of the South, no inconsiderable number of the former would be unable to survive very long.

Mr. Andrew Carnegie, the leading iron and steel maker of America, after his visit to the South last winter wrote a letter to the *Manufacturers' Record*, in which he said of Alabama furnaces: "$10 per ton cost for their foundry iron is a liberal estimate with good management, and for a series of years some of the best located and best managed furnaces may be able to do even better than this figure. But as far as I could see, the average cost of the district must be in the neighborhood of $10, everything counted. The ability to manufacture at this price must give the Southern manufacturers a large market for their pig iron. When the next stage comes, and they seek to manufacture the pig iron into more advanced forms, I believe it will be done by converting pig into steel by means of Bessemer and open hearth basic processes." This admission that the "average cost, everything counted," is about $10 a ton for foundry iron, will undoubtedly carry great weight, but there are furnaces in Alabama which make iron at probably not over $8.50 a ton.

In the early part of 1889, Mr. Abram S. Hewitt visited the South and expressed himself very freely and very enthusiastically over the future of its iron interests, and in an interview published in England during his visit there, said that it was possible to make iron in the South at $7.50 a ton.

In writing of the South's iron interests a few years ago, Col. A. K. McClure, of Philadelphia, said: * * * * * "It is idle for Pennsylvania and other great iron and coal-producing States to close their eyes to the fact that we have reached the beginning of a great revolution in those products. No legislation, no sound public policy, no sentiment can halt such a revolution when the immutable laws of trade command it; and the sudden tread of the hordes from the Northern forests upon ancient Rome did not more certainly threaten the majesty of the mistress of the world than does the tread of the iron and coal diggers of Alabama threaten the majesty of the Northern iron and coal fields. * * * These lessons come upon us plain as the noon-day sun, and it is mid-summer madness not to read them understandingly. We cannot war with destiny; we cannot efface the beneficent gifts of Him who leads the waters to the sea and sends them back in the dews and rains of Heaven. Alabama has been gifted far beyond even our boasted

empire of Pennsylvania, and only the Southern sluggard has hitherto
given the race to the North. Now there is a New South, with new
teachings, new opportunities, new energies, and manifestly a new destiny,
and the time is at hand when a large portion of the great iron and coal
products of the country which enter competing centers will be supplied
cheaper from Alabama than from any State in the North. How Pennsylvania will solve the problem I do not assume to decide, but the logical
result would be the transfer of the portion of the iron industry that can
best prosper here (in the South) from the North to the South, just as the
spinning and weaving of cotton must soon come to the cotton fields, and
the better water-power and climate which they furnish."

The iron makers of the South having established this industry upon
such a broad and solid basis as to fully convince the entire business
world of its permanency and magnitude, have for many months been
devoting very close study to the opportunities for steel making. They
are not content to confine their operations to producing pig iron and
leave to the North and the West the more desirable business of manufacturing steel. For a while it was claimed that the South had no ores
suitable for making Bessemer iron and steel, and would only be able to
engage in the manufacture of basic steel. Recent events have proved
that this is a mistake. There are practically unlimited supplies of high-
grade Bessemer ores in different parts of the South, and arrangements
have lately been matured for utilizing them on a large scale. The first
company actively organized to build a Bessemer plant south of Maryland was the North Carolina Steel & Iron Co., which was formed on
November 30th, 1889, with a capital stock of $1,000,000. This company
is composed of a number of leading capitalists, and some prominent
officers in Southern railroads. It purchased extensive Bessemer ore properties, besides several thousand acres of land at Greensboro, N. C., and at
this place expects to build furnaces to make Bessemer iron, and follow these
with a steel rail mill, rolling mill, &c. It is a conservative statement to say that North Carolina has Bessemer ores in sufficient quantity
to be practically inexhaustible for generations to come, though every
Bessemer furnace in the country were to draw its ore supplies from that
State. The future of the State as an iron-producing territory is exceedingly bright. The building of new railroads is opening up the mountainous regions where Bessemer ores are found in such abundance, and the
nearness of these ores to the Kentucky and Virginia coking coal fields
promises to give this territory exceptional advantages for producing
cheap iron and steel.

While greater attention has been attracted to the iron interests of Alabama than to those of any other Southern State, so much so that Alabama has steadily boasted that it could produce iron at a lower cost than any other section of the country, it is probable that there are favored points in other Southern States that can make iron as cheaply as the most favored spot in Alabama. In Western North Carolina, East Tennessee, Southwest Virginia and Southeastern Kentucky there are iron ores sufficient in quantity and quality to meet the requirements of the most exacting furnaceman. At many points the ores are of very high grade, suitable for Bessemer steel, and the ease and cheapness of mining them, and their proximity to the best coking coal fields in the country, the Cumberland Gap and Pocahontas regions, unite to make it possible to produce Bessemer steel at a price that will mean as great a revolution in the steel trade of the country as the development of Birmingham's iron interests effected in the pig iron trade. It is probably in this territory that the most marked activity will be seen in iron and steel matters during the next few years. The investigations of American and English experts opened the eyes of the country to the advantages possessed by Middlesborough, Ky., on the western side of this territory, for iron and steel making based on the abundance of high-grade ores within a few miles of the great coking coal districts of Southeastern Kentucky and Southwestern Virginia. On the eastern limit of this great region is the Bessemer steel enterprise at Greensboro, N. C. Between these two points there are vast resources of iron ore in close proximity to coking coals, and throughout that entire section there is great activity in the development of the iron interests.

In Llano county, Texas, there is Bessemer ore of remarkably high quality, analyzing in some cases 70 and 71 per cent. metallic iron. Investigations have been in progress for some time to determine the quantity, and these reports are so favorable, both as to quantity and quality, that arrangements are being made for very extensive operations for mining the ore, and also for converting it into iron and steel both at Llano and Denison. Members of the Standard Oil Company have been making careful investigations in this section, having in view the erection of large steel works at Denison, good coking coal being found near that town.

The development of the coal, iron and steel interests of Carolina, Virginia and Kentucky will in no way hurt Alabama or retard its growth, except by drawing some of the capital and energy that otherwise might seek the latter State. There is room enough for a rapid progress of all parts of the South, as shown elsewhere in this pamphlet.

The production of pig iron in net tons in the South for each year from 1880 to 1889, according to the official report of the American Iron and Steel Association was as follows :

STATES.	1880.	1881.	1882.	1883.	1884.	1885.	1886.	1887.	1888.	1889.
Maryland	61,437	48,756	54,524	49,153	27,312	17,299	30,502	37,427	17,606	33,847
Virginia	29,934	83,711	87,731	152,907	157,483	163,782	156,250	175,715	197,396	251,356
North Carolina	800	1,150		435	1,790	2,200	3,640	2,400	2,898
Georgia	27,321	37,401	42,364	45,364	42,655	32,924	46,490	40,917	39,397	27,559
Alabama	77,190	98,081	112,765	172,465	189,664	227,138	283,859	292,762	449,492	791,425
Texas	2,500	3,000	1,321	2,381	5,140	1,843	3,250	4,353	.....	4,544
West Virginia	70,338	66,409	73,220	88,398	55,231	69,007	98,618	82,311	95,259	117,900
Kentucky	57,708	45,973	66,522	54,629	45,052	37,553	54,844	41,907	56,790	42,518
Tennessee	70,873	87,406	137,602	133,963	134,597	101,199	199,166	250,344	267,931	294,655
Total										
Southern States	397,301	451,540	577,275	699,260	657,599	712,835	875,179	929,436	1,132,858	1,566,702

	1880.	1881.	1882.	1883.	1884.
Total Whole Country....	4,295,414	4,641,564	5,178,122	5,146,972	4,589,043
	1885.	1886.	1887.	1888.	1889.
	4,529,869	6,365,328	7,187,206	7,269,628	8,517,008

The most striking fact in connection with the output of iron in the two sections is brought out by comparing the production of 1887 and 1888, two years of dullness in the iron trade, and, as already said, it is during such periods as these that the South's advantages are made the more apparent. In 1887 the South produced 929,436 tons of iron, and in 1888 1,132,858 tons, a gain of 203,422 tons, while the North, which made 6,257,770 tons in 1887, made 6,136,770 tons in 1888, a decrease of 121,000 tons. Presented in tabular form this makes the following showing :

	1887 tons.	1888 tons.	
Production of Iron in the South	929,436	1,132,858	Increase, 203,422
In the rest of the country	6,257,770	6,136,770	Decrease, 121,000

As suggestive as these figures are, the margin of difference in the amount of iron produced in the two sections will rapidly narrow, as year after year the South, which is just on the threshold of its iron development, increases the number of its furnaces, while in the North many old furnaces are being abandoned and comparatively few new ones are being built. The production of iron in the South jumped from 1,132,858 tons in 1888, to 1,566,702 tons in 1889. A number of large new furnaces went into blast late in the year, and hence their output will be more noticeable in 1890, during which year the South will probably produce over 2,000,000 tons of iron.

In the ten years from 1880 to 1889 the South increased its iron output from 397,301 tons to 1,566,702 tons, while the gain in the rest of the country was from 3,898,113 to 6,950,366 tons. The percentage of increase was 294 in the South and 78 in the rest of the country. The South enters upon the new decade with every assurance of making a still better comparative showing at the end of 1899 than even this record of 1880-89.

There are now under contract to be built and under construction in the South about 30 furnaces. As nearly all of them are large they will average over 100 tons capacity a day or an aggregate capacity of over 1,000,000 tons a year. Some have imagined that the South would soon reach the limit of profitable iron production and have to stop building new furnaces, but this point is fully covered by a recent article in the Nashville Herald by Col. A. M. Shook, the manager of the Southern Iron Company of Nashville, who for twenty years has been one of the foremost iron makers of the country. Col. Shook says: "The feeling that there was great danger of an overproduction of pig iron, especially in the South, has been shared almost universally for the past three years by those who were most interested in its manufacture. This, too, was a most natural conclusion, based upon the conditions that existed at that time, and up to within six or eight months ago, the older pig iron producing sections, with, perhaps, the exception of the Hocking Valley, keeping up their annual production, and in some instances increasing it. The immense stocks on hand in England were also a constant menace to producers in this country.

What are the conditions as they exist to-day? Statistics of our production for 1889 show an increase of over 1,200,000 tons, and this is not based upon any abnormal railroad construction which always superinduces enormous consumption of iron and iron products. Notwithstanding this fact, this largely increased output has been consumed and our stocks to-day are no more than they were a year ago.

The production in Great Britain for 1889 was also larger than ever before, and it is now a conceded fact that the iron makers of that country have about reached the limit of their production ; and even the high price of iron, which is now prevalent, and which is nearly 100 per cent. higher than two years ago, is not largely affecting their production. Notwithstanding these high prices, their consumption has increased and is increasing enormously.

Now, if these facts are true is it not quite evident that there is no reason for having any alarm about the future of our iron market?

The outlook for business this year is infinitely better than it was a year ago, the business that is being offered to the railroads being greater than ever known before, and taken as a whole their earnings are larger. This indicates a universal degree of prosperity throughout the entire country, which made and consumed more than one million tons more iron in 1889 than was made in 1888, which was up to that time the largest production ever reached in this country. Is it not almost certain that we will increase our consumption in a greater ratio in 1890 than in 1889? And is it not also true that the result of the promised prosperity of 1890 will not be fully harvested until 1891? For these reasons I claim that we will have an exceptionally prosperous year in the iron business, not only during 1890, but that it will be even more so during 1891. Many railroad schemes that are now budding will simply get well under way during this year, and during next year the rails and equipment will have to be provided, which will necessitate a very much larger consumption of pig iron in 1891 than in 1890."

"The question," continued Col. Shook, "that naturally suggests itself is where is this largely increased output of pig iron to come from? No section of America is looking to any large new development in the iron business excepting the South—I mean by the South, southwest Virginia, western North Carolina, eastern Kentucky, east Tennessee, north Georgia and north Alabama, including the Birmingham iron district. This field can be made to produce all the iron wanted in this country for the next century. It seems that nature has provided this section with all the materials necessary to make pig iron, with a lavish hand. * * * When the fact is considered that, perhaps, in ten years this country will be required to produce 15,000,000 of tons of iron annually, and the further fact that that increased production must come largely from this field; that, in other words, the production of pig iron must be increased in this country from half a million to one million tons annually to keep pace with the increased consumption, it means that twenty or thirty large-sized furnaces will have to be built every year to keep up with the enlarged demand. No other section on this continent has the materials in such close proximity and such boundless quantities, together with the unusual facilities for transportation both by water and rail."

Or, in a few words, the natural increase in the consumptive requirements of this country must run from 500,000 to 1,000,000 tons annually, even without any special growth in iron and steel ship building industries and in the exporting of iron and steel, two lines of possible heavy consumption which seem to be absolutely assured. This increased demand must of necessity be met by the South.

That the full importance of the traffic which this iron business will afford to Southern railroads and its influence upon railroad construction in that section may be appreciated, some comparative statistics are given which will be found of interest. In making iron, the railroads handle about 5½ tons of freight, including the ore, coke and limestone carried to the furnace and the iron hauled away, for every ton of iron produced. On the basis of this exhibit 2,000,000 tons of iron, which is probably less than what the South's output in 1890 will be, would furnish 11,000,000 tons of freight, not counting any of the indirect traffic that would necessarily be developed by the growth of this business.   This 11,000,000 tons would mean 550,000 carloads of 40,000 pounds each.   It would mean a traffic more than six times as great in the number of tons as the entire cotton crop of the South, estimating that at 7,000,000 bales and 500 pounds to a bale. The influence of the wheat crop upon the railroads of the country is very sensibly felt, and especially in Wall street, where prices of railroad stocks constantly turn on the preliminary estimates as to the probable yield, and yet 400,000,000 bushels of wheat, which is but little short of the crop of 1888 for the entire country, would be only 12,000,000 tons, or but 1,000,-000 tons more than the tonnage of the South's estimated iron business of 1890.   The immensity of 11,000,000 tons of freight cannot probably be more forcibly impressed upon the mind than by the mere statement that if it were to be shipped by water its transportation would furnish 3,000-ton cargoes to over 3,600 ocean steamships.

It has already been said that the South is building factories and shops of various sorts so rapidly that the consumption of pig iron there will be very greatly increased.   This point is scarcely appreciated by the Northern people, who have heard so much about new furnaces that they have overlooked the new rolling mills, car works, pipe works, stove foundries, machine works, agricultural implement factories and kindred enterprises. Comparatively few outside of Virginia know that in Roanoke, a town which was but a small way-station five or six years ago, there are car and locomotive works which employ 1,200 hands, and which not only build rolling stock for Southern roads, but compete with Northern works for furnishing cars to Northern railroads, and that Richmond has locomotive building works which cost $800,000 to construct and equip.   As we go South other enterprises of fully as great magnitude are found in a number of places which have grown up since the development of the iron trade commenced.   In the older places, such as Richmond, Louisville, Knoxville, Nashville, Chattanooga, Memphis and many others, there are many iron industries, the trade of which is steadily expanding.   These are already known.   When we come to the newer towns, the ones that have attracted the greatest attention as builders of new furnaces, the magnitude of the diversified iron enterprises is seen.   Birmingham's rolling mills have pushed their product even into the Chicago market ; its stove works have furnished stoves to Mexico ; its pin and tack factory ships its goods in all directions, while car works and machine shops help to swell the home consumption of the iron which its many furnaces produce. This rapidly increasing diversity of Southern industrial growth is seen from Maryland to Texas, and is being forcibly illustrated in Birmingham, in Chattanooga, in Atlanta, in Florence, in Roanoke, in Middlesborough and elsewhere.

It is not a one-sided and hence an unstable growth, but is a well-rounded development, covering every phase of this great industry, from the mining of the ore to its conversion into pig iron, and thence through all stages of progress until it is turned out as the finished product. The far-reaching influence which this rapidly growing industry must inevitably exert upon all the business interests—railroad, financial, commercial and industrial—of the entire country must command thoughtful study. It is not within the scope of this article to attempt to portray that. The aim of the writer has been simply to present in as brief a manner as possible the most striking features of the South's iron industry, to show on what its growth is based, the profitableness of the business when well managed, and the magnitude which it is now assuming as the fires of one great furnace after another are lighted.

THE RAPID INCREASE IN COAL MINING.

The magnitude of the wealth of the South in coal is beyond computation. The entire coal area of Great Britain covers 11,900 square miles, while West Virginia alone has 16,000 square miles of coal fields; Alabama, 8,660 square miles; Kentucky, nearly 13,000; Tennessee, 5,100, Arkansas, over 9,000, and other Southern States considerable coal areas. Moreover, the coal is easily and cheaply mined, and is, as to much of it, of the best quality. Some idea of how nearly inexhaustible are the coal beds of the South may be gained from a few statistics as to the Warrior coal fields of Alabama, which is simply one of the coal fields of one State. Regarding the Warrior field, Prof. Henry McCalley, in his late geological report, says that it "contains about 7,800 square miles, and is about two-thirds as large as the entire coal territory of Great Britain. Its coal measures are over 3,000 feet thick, containing fifty-three seams of coal, being from a few inches to fourteen feet thick, having a combined thickness of over 125 feet of pure coal. It is estimated that they contain not less than 113,119,000,000 tons, of which about 108,394,000,000 tons would be available. The coal is valued now at about $150,000,000,000 at the mine, of which $30,000,000,000 would be profit, being about 200 times the present total assessed value of the property in Alabama, and would buy every foot of Alabama territory at $900 per acre. These coals, like those of other fields in Alabama, are especially enhanced in value owing to the proximity of vast deposits of red and brown iron ores and limestones."

Nowhere else, so far as is known, are the coal fields so admirably located in relation to iron ore, to the best markets and as regards the ease and cheapness of mining, as in the South. The wide mineral belt, which extends from Wheeling and Harper's Ferry, W. Va., to Northern Alabama, has greater undeveloped wealth and a greater combination of advantages and possibilities of development than any other area of equal extent in the world. This belt includes a large part of the two Virginias, the Carolinas, Kentucky, Tennessee, Georgia and Alabama. As rapid as has been the expansion of the coal mining industry of this section it is but in its incipiency and of very small proportions compared with what will be seen within the next five or ten years. The production of coal in each Southern State in 1880, 1882, 1887, 1888 and 1889 was as follows :

	1880.	1882.	1887.	1888.	†1889.
Maryland..........	2,228,917	1,294,310	3,278,023	3,476,479	3,213,886
Virginia.......	15,800	100,000	825,263	1,073,071	1,592,385
West Virginia......	1,830,845	2,900,000	4,882,820	5,398,500	4,726,047
Georgia..........	154,043	175,000	313,714	230,000	205,000
Alabama.......... ..	323,072	800,000	1,900,000	2,240,000	3,000,000
Tennessee..........	495,134	881,000	1,900,000	1,917,000	2,500,000
Arkansas	14,778	50,000	150,000	193,000	250,000
Texas......	....	....	75,000	90,000	200,000
Kentucky	946,288	1,300,000	1,933,385	2,570,270	3,750,000
Total	6,049,471	6,519,316	15,212,006	18,001,270	19,497,418

†These figures were compiled by Mr. F. E. Saward, editor Coal Trade Journal, N. Y.

In 1882 the South produced 6,569,316 tons of coal, and in 1889 19,497,-418 tons. Thus in 7 years, from 1882 to 1889 the output of Southern coal mines advanced from 6,500,000 tons to upwards of 19,500,000 tons. Between the taking of the census of 1880 and that of 1890 the output of Southern coal mines has more than trebled, and every year will show continued gains as the development of this industry is rapidly expanding.

In southwest Virginia, in West Virginia and in southeastern Kentucky the abundance of coking coals of superior quality has caused an almost unprecedented activity in the mining and coke making interests of that section.

Some idea of the extent of the operations that are being carried on in this district may be gained from the fact that the American Association, Limited, which owns about 60,000 acres of coal lands in the neighborhood of the new town of Middlesborough, Ky., has within the last twelve months made leases of coal properties for mining to fourteen different operators. It is claimed that these mines alone will put out 1,500,000 tons of coal within eighteen months. Many new mines besides these on the American Association's lands are being opened in the same part of Kentucky, and in Virginia and West Virginia there is similar activity. In Alabama the demand for coal exceeds the output, notwithstanding the rapid increase in the production, and extensive arrangements are in progress for increasing the capacity of mines now in operation and for opening new mines.

SOME FACTS ABOUT COTTON.

EIGHT BILLION DOLLARS DRAWN TO THE SOUTH SINCE 1865 TO PAY FOR COTTON.

Cotton is one of the most remarkable products that enters into the world's commercial and industrial interests. Its production gives the South a very great advantage over any other section of the country. Cotton is always in demand, and its consumption is steadily on the increase. The simple fact that since 1865 nearly $8,000,000,000 have been brought into the South to pay for cotton explains in part the marvelous recuperative powers of this section since the war. While bad agricultural methods have made cotton raising unprofitable to many farmers, yet there is no question but that cotton is one of the most profitable crops that can be raised when its cultivation is carried on intelligently on a cash basis. Southern farmers who raise their own foodstuffs, making cotton their surplus money crop, find it a very profitable one, and almost invariably become well-to-do financially.

The South produces about three-fourths of the world's annual cotton crop, but manufactures only about seven or eight per cent. of what it raises, the balance furnishing the material for work for millions of spindles in New England and in Europe. The total cotton crop of the world now runs from about 10,000,000 to 11,000,000 bales, of which the South raises on an average, of late years, 7,000,000 bales. Upwards of 80,000,000 spindles are in operation in the world, and of this number the South has but 2,000,000, but it should be remembered that in 1880 the South had only 660,000 spindles. The increase in the number of its spindles has been surprisingly great, and the future promises still more rapid growth.

Some facts regarding the production of cotton, its value, and the amount exported will prove of interest.

COTTON TRADE OF THE UNITED STATES SINCE 1865.

Crop years from July 1 to August 31	Acreage.	Total crop. bales.	Total value.	Consumption in U.S. bales.	For'gn Exports. bales.	Value of Exports.
1865-1866	....	2,269,316	$432,331,139	666,100	1,554,664	$281,385,223
1866-1867	....	2,097,254	294,159,007	770,030	1,557,054	201,470,423
1867-1868	....	2,519,554	278,618,580	906,036	1,655,816	152,820,733
1868-1869	....	2,366,467	304,810,362	926,375	1,465,880	162,633,052
1869-1870	....	3,122,551	329,466,391	865,160	2,206,480	227,027,624
1870-1871	....	4,352,317	326,061,036	1,110,196	3,169,909	218,327,109
1871-1872	8,911,000	2,974,351	274,569,592	1,237,330	1,957,314	180,684,595
1872-1873	9,560,000	3,930,508	333,278,121	1,201,127	2,679,986	227,243,069
1873-1874	10,816,000	4,170,338	310,063,419	1,305,943	2,840,981	211,223,580
1874-1875	10,982,000	3,832,991	272,177,136	1,193,005	2,684,708	190,638,625
1875-1876	11,635,000	4,632,313	399,445,168	1,351,870	3,234,244	192,659,255
1876-1877	11,500,000	4,474,069	252,602,340	1,428,013	3,030,835	171,118,508
1877-1878	11,825,000	4,773,865	255,768,165	1,489,022	3,360,254	180,031,484
1878-1879	12,240,000	5,074,155	236,586,031	1,558,329	3,481,004	162,304,250
1879-1880	12,680,000	5,761,252	313,696,452	1,789,978	3,885,003	211,535,905
1880-1881	16,123,000	6,605,750	356,524,911	1,938,937	4,589,346	247,695,786
1881-1882	16,851,000	5,456,048	304,298,744	1,964,535	3,582,622	199,812,644
1882-1883	16,276,000	6,949,756	327,938,137	2,073,096	4,766,597	224,921,413
1883-1884	16,780,000	5,713,200	288,803,902	1,876,683	3,916,581	197,984,295
1884-1885	17,426,000	5,706,165	287,253,972	1,753,125	3,947,972	198,744,802
1885-1886	18,379,444	6,575,691	313,723,080	2,162,544	4,336,203	206,879,697
1886-1887	18,581,012	6,505,087	298,504,215	2,111,532	4,453,020	205,243,843
1887-1888	18,961,897	7,046,833	336,433,653	2,257,247	4,627,502	220,928,551
1888-1889	19,058,591	6,938,290	†350,000,000	2,314,091	4,742,347	237,775,270
1889-1890	....	†7,250,000	†390,000,000	....	......	†250,000,000
Total....			$7,867,113,555			$5,161,989,736

†Estimated.

These figures are somewhat startling in their magnitude. They show that the aggregate value of the cotton raised in the South since 1865 has been over $7,800,000,000, and that the value of cotton exported to foreign countries during the same period has been $5,161,000,000. The great influence which cotton has exerted upon the foreign commerce of the United States can be readily appreciated from these statistics.

It may be asked if $7,800,000,000 of outside money has gone South since 1865 to pay for cotton, what has been accomplished, and why is the South still comparatively poor? The answer is that the condition of the agricultural interests of this section after the war, due to the extreme poverty of the people at the close of that disastrous struggle, to the system of securing money in advance by mortgaging the cotton to be raised, the exorbitant rates of interest, the purchase of necessity of farm and house supplies on credit at from 75 to 80 per cent. more than cash prices, all tended to consume the entire profits on the production of cotton. Until very recently these conditions were against the raising at home of corn, bacon and other necessities, and almost the entire aggregate received for cotton went back to the North for foodstuffs. The lack of manufactures necessitated dependence upon other sections for almost every line of manufactured goods, from a pin to a locomotive. A careful study of the history of this section will show that the South was not to blame, except to a limited extent, for this condition of affairs. Gradually the people rallied from the disasters of war and commenced the development of manufactures and the diversification of their farm products. Their "smoke house and corn crib" have ceased to be in the West, and the South is now nearly self-supporting in supplying its consumptive requirements of foodstuffs. Cotton is yearly becoming more and more a surplus crop, and the several hundred millions of dollars which it annually yields will, in the future, largely remain here for the enrichment of this section, instead of going North and West to pay for bacon, breadstuffs and manufactured goods. In this change there is a revolution in the currents of business that must produce surprising results. Added to the one or two hundred millions of dollars of cotton money that have for twenty-five years annually gone North, but which will now remain in the South, will be an equal, or possibly a greater amount brought to the South to pay for the iron, the lumber and the cotton goods that are now being shipped North, the millions that will come to pay for mineral and timber lands, the $50,000,000 or more that is now paid for early vegetables and fruits, and the great aggregate, reaching probably already $25,000,000 spent by winter visitors who come South to enjoy its climate. These facts are astounding. They can but impress anyone with the mighty change that is now being wrought out in the condition of the South.

That the South, which produces the cotton, is destined to manufacture it admits of no questioning. The South has the natural advantages necessary for success in this business, and whatever difficulties there may be in the way are easily overcome when practical experience, backed by capital, is brought to bear upon the matter. There may be times of depression, but this will not stop the sure and steady growth of this great industry. Good operatives, it has been said by some, cannot be had in the South, and this section can never hope, so some of our New England friends claim, to do anything more than manufacture coarse goods. But a few years ago the same people were just as ready to claim that cotton manufacturing, even of coarse goods, would never amount to much in the South. Forced now to admit that Southern mills control this branch of the business, they fall back on the threadbare argument against the possibility of the Southern mills ever successfully competing with New England mills on the finer goods. Before many years have passed they will be forced to abandon this. Every cotton mill that goes into operation in the South helps to make more certain the future supremacy of this section in every branch of this industry. With the increase in this business the number of trained operatives increases, and the skill necessary for the production of finer goods will be found ready at hand when the cotton manufacturers of the South decide that the time has come for devoting more attention to fine goods.

It was but a few years ago when the statement that the South would, in time, control the iron market of the country was ridiculed, and the reply made that, while the South might produce a large quantity of low grade pig iron, it could never hope to compete with the North in the finer, finished products of iron and steel, where an abundance of capital and skilled mechanics would enable that section to still control this branch of the business. At first the South demonstrated that it could make pig iron more cheaply than any other part of this country. Having done this, attention was turned to the building of enterprises for producing the finished goods, and locomotive works, car and car-wheel works, tack factories, stove foundries, hardware factories, nail mills, engine works, saw factories and hundreds of kindred enterprises are daily proving that the South can manufacture every variety of fine products requiring the highest skilled labor. As in iron, so it will be in cotton. When the time is ripe, and that time seems to be at hand, for the South to turn its attention to finer qualities of cotton goods, it will do so, and do it successfully.

In 1880 the census reported $207,781,868 invested in cotton manufacture in the United States, and the consumption of cotton by American mills 1,570,342 bales, or much less than one-fourth of an average crop. On this basis it would require an investment of over $800,000,000 in mills to consume our entire cotton crop; so we can form some idea of what the magnitude of the cotton manufacturing interests is. Out of an estimated total of 80,000,000 spindles in the world, the United States has only about 13,000,000, Great Britain having over one-half, or 42,000,000.

The *Manufacturers' Record* lately compiled, through special reports from cotton mills in the South, a list of all the mills in that section, with the number of spindles and looms in each; and, comparing these figures with the reports of the census of 1880, we have the following interesting table, showing a most remarkable increase:

States.	July 31, 1889.			May, 1880.		
	No. of Mills.	No. of Spindles.	No. of Looms.	No. of Mills.	No. of Spindles.	No. of Looms.
Alabama	21	131,904	2,414	16	49,432	863
Arkansas	5	13,800	224	2	2,015	28
Florida	1	1,400	....	1	816	....
Georgia	73	455,998	10,246	40	198,656	4,493
Kentucky	6	45,200	677	3	9,022	73
Louisiana	5	60,280	1,584	2	6,096	120
Maryland	25	175,642	3,536	19	125,706	2,425
Mississippi	11	69,396	2,054	8	18,568	644
North Carolina	111	386,837	7,851	49	92,385	1,790
South Carolina	44	417,730	10,687	14	82,334	1,676
Tennessee	31	126,324	12,478	16	35,736	818
Texas	8	50,868	496	2	2,648	71
Virginia	14	99,889	2,754	8	44,340	1,322
Total	355	2,035,268	45,001	161	667,854	14,323

These figures show that the number of mills now in the South as compared with 1880 has doubled, while the number of spindles and looms has more than trebled, the tendency being to build mills of greater capacity than formerly. From 161 mills having 667,854 spindles and 14,323 looms in 1880 this industry has increased until there are now 355 mills with 2,035,268 spindles and 45,001 looms in the South. As remarkable as is this increase, these figures really do not fully represent the development of this business, for they do not include the spindles and looms of many new mills now under construction, and others upon which work will shortly begin.

The foregoing table shows that Georgia leads in the number of spindles, having 455,998, while South Carolina is first in the number of looms and second in the number of spindles. South Carolina is probably making not only more rapid progress in the development of this industry than any other Southern State, but its advance in that line seems to be more evenly rounded out, and on a broader basis looking to the future. Its mills are very large, and many of them have grown to their present size from small beginnings, through wise management. They have paid good dividends for years, and steadily increased their surplus, investing it in new machinery and new mills. They have, moreover, apparently given closer study to the possibility of diversity and of the making of finer goods.

The importance of developing this industry cannot be too strongly emphasized. It keeps at home the great wealth produced in manufacturing the South's leading staple. As already shown on the basis of the capital invested and the bales of cotton consumed in American mills in 1880, an investment of $800,000,000 would be required to manufacture the entire cotton crop of this country. Instead of selling for about $350,000,000 a year, as the cotton crop now does, it would, if wholly manufactured in the South, represent over $1,000,000,000 a year. Cotton mills furnish employment to a large class of labor that must remain idle for lack of work, except as this business grows. In every town and city of the South there are hundreds, and in some thousands, of white women and girls anxious to work, while there is no work for them. Given employment at cotton manufacturing, in which they readily become expert, they are enabled to support themselves, and thus to add greatly to the wealth of the community. Mr. John Hill, one of the leading cotton manufacturing experts of the South, has estimated that, of the operatives given employment by the establishment of a cotton mill, at least 80 or 90 per cent. are people who before had been unemployed, and hence had added nothing to the productive or wealth-creating power of the State. Formerly idlers—not from choice, but from force of circumstances, they cease to be a drain on others and become self-supporting. This is one of the great blessings which the growth of cotton manufacturing brings to the South.

Hon. Edward Atkinson, of Boston, the well-known political economist, in his report for the census upon the cotton manufacturing interests of the country, after showing the much greater advantages that New England possesses for this industry as compared with the most favored districts of England, wrote :

" It may be said that this proves too much, and that the cotton spinners of the Southern States will have the same relative advantage over New England. Let this be freely admitted. We are treating the question of the future supremacy of the United States in the manufacture as well as the growth of cotton, and if the future changes in population, wealth and condition of the different sections of this country shall cause the increase of spindles, especially in the coarse fabrics, to be planted in the healthy hill country of northern Georgia, eastern Tennessee and the Carolinas, it will simply be the greater evidence that natural laws are paramount. If Georgia has twice the advantages over Lancashire that New England now possesses, it will only be the fault of the people of Georgia if they do not reap the benefit of it."

The force of Mr. Atkinson's logic will assuredly be seen in the not very distant future. Georgia, the Carolinas and Tennessee will not monopolize this industry. The whole South will share in its development, and while Georgia and the Carolinas have of late years made the greatest progress, the other States are following very fast in the same line of progress.

A leading New England cotton mill builder, Mr. C. R. Makepeace, of Providence, R. I., in a recent letter to the *Manufacturers' Record* on the advantages of the South for cotton manufacturing, said :

" It is well known that the true interests of a people are best promoted when the products of their industries, either for domestic or foreign trade, are of the kind most favored by nature and produced where nature affords the greatest facilities for cheap production. It is of interest to note that the advantages claimed by the mills in the North over those in the South are precisely the same as those claimed by the mills of Great Britain over the mills of New England several years ago, but which the manufacturers of New England have proven to be untrue in the main. That Great Britain does possess some slight advantage over New England in this branch of industry is true as the North possesses certain advantages over the South and will continue to do so.

"The mills of the Southern States possess a decided advantage over the mills in the North and Great Britain in that they have the raw cotton at their doors, and that this alone represents a money value sufficient to give them control of the coarse goods has been fully demonstrated within the last ten years. This difference can be more clearly shown by the following illustration : Let us assume a 40,000 spindle mill is located at any well selected site in the cotton growing section of the Southern States. This mill, properly equipped with the latest and most approved style of machinery for the manufacture of standard 4-4 sheetings to Nos. 12 to 14 yarns, would cost complete $800,000 and would consume 20,000 bales of cotton per annum. It is variously estimated that the difference in cost of a bale of cotton—490 pounds—between the mills in Augusta, Ga., and Fall River, Mass., is from $4 to $6 a bale. Assume the lowest estimate of $4 per bale and you have 20,000x$4 equals $80,000 in favor of the Augusta mill, or a saving of 10 per cent. on the complete cost of the mill, in cotton alone."

IN AGRICULTURE THE SOUTH LEADS.

A MARVELOUS RECORD OF PROGRESS MADE BY SOUTHERN FARMERS.

The industrial development of the South has attracted so much attention that no one will question its magnitude, but there are few who realize the extent of the progress made of late years by the agricultural interests of this section. It is the combination of increasing agricultural prosperity and industrial activity which has placed the South in its present favorable financial condition. It will be well to show by statistics what the farmers have done since 1870. The production of leading crops in 1870, 1887, 1888 and 1889 in the South was :

	1870.	1887.	1888.	1889.	Increase in 1889 over 1870.
Cotton, bales...........	3,011,996	7,017,707	6,938,290	† 7,250,000	4,238,004
Corn, bushels...	249,072,118	492,415,000	509,705,000	519,517,000	270,444,882
Wheat, bushels........	33,341,340	52,384,000	44,207,000	55,060,000	21,718,660
Oats, bushels.........	31,973,542	81,506,000	78,254,000	77,714,000	45,740,458

† Estimated.

From 3,000,000 bales of cotton in 1870, the yield in the South advanced to 7,250,000 bales in 1889. Thus it has largely more than doubled its cotton crop. Better still, it increased its corn production from 249,000,000 bushels in 1870 to 519,517,000 in 1889, a gain of 270,000,000 bushels. In wheat the South's increase in 1889 over 1870 was nearly 22,000,000 bushels.

and in oats the South increased from 31,970,000 bushels in 1870 to 77,714,-
000 bushels in 1889, a gain of 45,000,000 bushels. It is since 1879 or 1880,
however, that the South has made the most marked agricultural progress.
The yield of principal crops in the South in 1879, 1887, 1888 and 1889
was as follows :

Crops.	1879.	1887.	1888.	1889.
Cotton, bales	5,755,359	7,017,000	6,938,290	† 7,250,000
Corn, bushels	333,121,290	492,415,000	509,705,000	519,517,000
Wheat, bushels	54,476,740	52,384,000	44,207,000	55,060,000
Oats, bushels	43,476,600	81,506,000	78,254,000	77,714,000
Total grain, bushels	431,074,630	626,305,000	632,166,000	652,291,000

Increase over 1879—	Cotton, bales.	Grain, bushels.
In 1889	1,494,641	221,216,370
In 1888	1,244,641	201,091,370
In 1887	1,261,641	195,230,370

† Estimated.

These figures show an increase in the production of grain from 1879
to 1888 of over 220,000,000 bushels. How does this increase compare
with the production in the rest of the country ? The following figures
show :

Yield in whole country, except the South.	1879.	1887.	1888.	1889.
Corn, bushels	1,214,780,500	963,746,000	1,478,085,000	1,593,375,000
Wheat, bushels	394,279,890	403,945,000	371,661,000	435,500,000
Oats, bushels	320,293,720	578,112,000	623,481,000	673,801,000
Total	1,929,354,110	1,945,803,000	2,473,227,000	2,702,676,000

Notwithstanding the fact that the West produced last year the
largest corn crop ever made, the increase as compared with 1879 was only
31 per cent., while the increase in the South's corn crop from 1879 to 1889
was 55 per cent.

While the South, as shown by the foregoing figures, made an increase
from 1879 to 1887 of 195,000,000 bushels of grain, or 45 per cent., the increase in all the rest of the country for the same period was only 16,000,-
000 bushels, or less than one per cent. It is true that the West had a
short corn crop that year, but so did Kentucky, one of the largest of the
corn-producing States of the South, and moreover the West had an
unusually large crop of oats, the largest, in fact, ever produced up to
that time. But if we were to give the North and West the benefit of the
large corn years of 1884, 1885 and 1886, and take as a comparison the
average crop for five years, the rate of increase in grain production for
the whole country, excepting the South, from 1870 to 1887, would still be
only about 12 per cent., against a 45 per cent. increase in the South. In
1888 the West had phenomenally large corn and oat crops, and the
increase over 1879 was very large, but the percentage of gain was only
28 per cent., while for the same time the South made an increase of 46
per cent. Thus the South, burdened by its weight of poverty entailed

by the war, with a disorganized labor system, and without immigration, except to Texas, has, since 1870, considerably more than doubled its cotton and grain crops, and made, surprising as it is, a much greater percentage of increase in the production of corn since 1879 than all the rest of the country. When we consider the poverty of the South at the start, and the lack of immigration, and contrast it with the wealth of the North and West, and the tremendous immigration to the agricultural regions of the West, this agricultural progress of the South is astonishing. It is a monument to the energy of the people of this section.

A comparison of the yield of corn by States in the South in 1879 and 1889 will show how general has been the advance:

	1879. Bushels.	1889. Bushels.
Maryland	13,721,000	15,105,000
Virginia	19,957,600	34,231,000
North Carolina	25,678,500	33,050,000
South Carolina	9,702,000	18,310,000
Georgia	20,627,400	33,730,000
Florida	1,945,650	5,206,000
Alabama	25,403,300	33,944,000
Mississippi	24,926,400	29,474,000
Louisiana	12,592,500	18,949,000
Texas	29,198,000	83,698,000
Arkansas	22,432,800	42,608,000
Tennessee	50,897,500	80,831,000
West Virginia	11,302,600	15,199,000
Kentucky	64,736,000	75,382,000
Total	333,121,250	519,517,000

A comparison of the value of live stock in the South in 1879, and on January 1, 1889, will prove of interest:

	1879.	1889.
Horses	$127,502,759	$168,082,001
Mules	65,059,675	117,178,894
Milch cows	47,630,990	69,515,924
Oxen and other cattle	87,019,999	133,919,075
Sheep	19,262,888	17,239,517
Hogs	44,935,943	63,226,139
Total	$391,412,254	$569,161,550
Increase		$177,749,296

This is a pretty healthy increase in the value of live stock between 1879 and 1889.

The total values of the chief agricultural products of the South for 1879 and 1889 (omitting sugar, rice, fruits and vegetables, &c., the value of which is not given in the United States Agricultural Department's reports) compare as follows:

	1879.	1889.
Cotton	$227,893,000	† $390,000,000
Corn	187,958,752	221,476,502
Wheat	65,575,378	44,701,792
Oats	20,193,011	28,763,002
Potatoes, barley, hay, tobacco, &c	69,478,313	100,000,000
Total	$571,098,454	$784,941,296
Increase		$213,842,842

†Partly estimated.

If to these figures we add the increase in fruits, vegetables, &c., the total gain in the value of agricultural products of the South in 1889 over 1879 was upwards of $250,000,000, while during the same time the increase in the value of live stock was, as has already been shown, $177,749,000. The crops of 1889 in the South were the largest ever raised. It is estimated that the cotton yield will reach 7,250,000 bales, and the corn crop was 519,517,000 bushels. Of fruits and vegetables, such crops as the South produced in 1889 were beyond anything known before in that section, and many millions of dollars were drawn from the North and West to pay for early Southern fruits and market produce. A conservative estimate would place the aggregate value of the South's agricultural products in 1889 at not less than $850,000,000.

RAILROADS.

THE SOUTH THE CENTER OF ACTIVITY IN RAILROAD BUILDING.

Although the mineral resources of the South and its vast forests have attracted widespread attention and drawn millions of dollars of capital to this section for investment, yet the development of its railroad interests has received still greater consideration and absorbed even more money.

"This," says a recent writer, "is the most commanding theatre of capital, and strikes the eye of the world not only for its colossal combinations of money, but the prestige of its participants. The capitalists of Europe and the United States, who have been so largely interested in building new railroads and improving old ones throughout the whole South, have added untold and incomputable momentum to the progress of that section. While they may not have led the way in starting the South on her wonderful speed of development, they have largely added to and confirmed—sealed, as it were—the confidence of the civilized world in the eligibility of the South as a field for investment and enterprise ; and the South owes an immense debt of gratitude to these monetary magnates who have stamped with the golden seal of their capital the indelible impress of their confidence. The logic of confidence in the South's progress is enunciated in the golden argument of capital, and is voiced in the fierce rhetoric of thunderous and clattering railroad trains. And these roads are bands of iron to bind our union in the bonds of indissoluble fraternity ; and the cogency of common interest is added to the kindliest friendship."

The magnitude of the investments made in Southern railroads since the first of January, 1880, is almost beyond comprehension. In nine years

20,000 miles of new road, not counting sidings and switches, have been laid in the fourteen Southern States. In 1880 the South had 26,612 miles of road, while at the end of 1889 it had 40,521. The gain has been nearly 100 per cent., while from 1880 to 1889 the gain in the whole country was only about 64 per cent.

In 1886 the South built 20 per cent. of the total new mileage of that year ; in 1887 it built 23 per cent.; in 1888 35 per cent., and during 1889 40 per cent. These facts indicate how rapidly the South is gaining in railroad construction as compared with the rest of the country. That the railroad mileage of the South has made a larger percentage of gain than the West, is an astonishing fact, in view of the tremendous growth of the great West, to which the millions of foreign immigrants that have landed in this country have mainly gone. The South, with but little immigration, and not yet fully recovered from the poverty entailed by the most disastrous war in the history of the world, is making a greater rate of progress in railroad building than even the rich and powerful West. In 1880 the total mileage of the country was 98,296 miles, and of this 20,562 miles, or 20 per cent. were in the South, while in 1889 the South had 40,-521 miles out of a total of 161,270, or 25 per cent.

The average cost of construction and equipment is not less than $25,-000 a mile, and at this rate the 20,000 miles of new road built since January 1st, 1880, represent a cash investment of $500,000,000.

The amount invested in building new roads is, however, but a part of the full sum expended during the last ten years in Southern railroad development. Old roads have been improved at a great outlay. Thousands of miles of iron rails have been replaced with steel, new and better bridges have been built, the rolling stock has been increased to meet the ever increasing volume of freight and passenger traffic, and other improvements made, the whole aggregating probably not far from half as much as the cost of the new roads constructed. Poor's Railroad Manual, the standard authority on such matters, gives the actual cost by States of all railroads in the country and their equipment, showing a total for the South in 1888 of over $1,400,000,000, against $679,000,000 in 1880, or an increase of about $721,000,000, to which may be added $50,000,000 or more for 1889, making the amount expended in the development of Southern railroads in the last ten years about $800,000,000.

All indications point to the greatest activity in railroad construction in the South during the next few years that has ever been seen in this section. So great is the increase in the volume of freight, that there is scarcely a road in the South that is not blocked with business, and the double tracking of nearly all leading Southern roads is becoming a pressing necessity.

The future of Southern railroad interests is very promising. The traffic will develop faster than facilities can be provided for handling it, and the prosperity of the South means the prosperity of its railroads. The railroad mileage by States in the South at the end of 1880 and 1889 was as follows :

States.	1880. Mileage.	1889. Mileage.
Maryland and D. C....	1,040	1,214
Virginia...	1,893	3,188
West Virginia	691	1,330
North Carolina	1,486	2,793
South Carolina	1,427	2,127
Georgia	2,459	4,277
Florida	518	2,433
Alabama	1,843	3,116
Mississippi	1,127	2,417
Louisiana	652	1,615
Arkansas... ..	859	2,112
Texas	3,244	8,494
Tennessee.	1,843	2,651
Kentucky	1,530	2,754
Total	20,612	40,521

THE SOUTH'S INCREASING FOREIGN COMMERCE.

A very striking fact in connection with the general growth of the South is the great increase in the foreign commerce of every Southern port during 1889. From the official statistics of the Bureau of Statistics the following figures have been compiled :

Ports.	Value of foreign exports for 1889.	1888.
Baltimore	$ 62,091,733	$ 45,104,613
Beaufort. S. C	1,106,296	849,839
Brazos, Texas	818,726	726,273
Brunswick, Ga	8,200,273	4,617,903
Charleston, S. C	16,355,933	13,003,628
Corpus Christi	2,653,832	1,952,812
Fernandina	316,458	176,377
Galveston	23,836,075	14,496,669
Key West	....	438,056
Mobile	3,918,266	3,442,619
New Orleans..	101,328,375	80,906,145
Newport News	6,373,606	6,281,664
Norfolk.....	12,802,334	13,812,641
Pearl River, Miss	1,091,949	851,586
Pensacola. Fla	3,705,404	2,691,268
Richmond	10,592,744	8,852,728
Saluria, Texas	1,407,824	1,325,122
Savannah	27,604,404	17,850,223
Teche, La	16,846	3,238
Wilmington, N. C	6,319,218	6,198,144
Total	$290,540,296	$223,581,558
Increase in 1889 over 1888	$ 66,958,738	.

The total increase for the whole country was $135,489,323, and of this gain the South had nearly one-half. The percentage of increase in the South was 29, against 14 in the balance of the country. These figures are extremely gratifying to all interested in the progress of the South. They show that its commerce is keeping even step in the march of progress with its industrial interests. While the South's foreign commerce has been growing so rapidly, as shown by these figures, its coastwise trade has developed probably with still greater rapidity, though there are no sources of exact statistical information on the subject.

TEN YEARS OF BANKING.

THE SOUTH LEADS IN THE RATE OF INCREASE IN NATIONAL BANKING.

A substantial business community must have a substantial banking system. Hence, to ascertain the stability of any community, one naturally turns to its banks first to see what their standing is.

Immediately following the war came the development and settlement of the great empire of the West. Immigrants from the overcrowded shops and fields of Europe entered our ports by the thousands every week, and pushed the line of civilization westward until the Mississippi river, which a few years before was an unexplored stream, became a most familiar highway. Railroads reached out into virgin prairies, which in a night, as it were, became dotted with farming communities. More roads were built to keep up with the streams of new settlers until the Rocky mountains were reached. Here the farming communities ended, but mining communities took up the rush, and by the aid of more railways soon brought the Pacific slope into close communication with the Mississippi valley. This immense development brought increased volumes of trade to the workshops and factories of New England. Modest little industrial plants added new buildings and machinery to supply the demands of these new settlements in the West in clothing the people, extending railways and supplying agricultural and other implements and utensils. Such an enormous traffic demanded the assistance of banking institutions, and much of the heaps of wealth that this great traffic brought into New England was used to establish banks and other financial institutions, which still further aided in developing the West.

Ten years after this great empire was thrown open to the world the demand for manufactures led to the establishment of many industries nearer the field of demand, and with the increase of manufacturing came the necessity for banking institutions. The marvelous growth of the

West and the multiplying of national banks there during the decade ending in 1879 does not directly concern us.

Meantime, how fared the South? Recuperative nature obliterated much of the devastation of war, landowners adjusted themselves to the new system of labor, the rich natural resources of the region became known to the world, numerous industries sprang up, railroads felt their way slowly but surely through mountain defiles and over rich, rolling bottom lands, and an era of prosperity began to dawn which, now that it is fairly under way, promises to be even more marvelous than was that in the great West.

The condition of the national banking system in 1879 well illustrates the true business situation in that year. In the whole country were 2,048 banks. Eleven hundred and sixty-six of these were in the North, which includes the New England States, New York, New Jersey, Pennsylvania and Delaware. In the West, which had at this time reached a high state of development, were 660 banks. This includes the States from Ohio on the east to Kansas and Nebraska on the West and Missouri and the Ohio river on the south. In the Southern States south of the Ohio and westward to, and including Arkansas and Texas, were 220 banks. It will thus be seen that the North had nearly twice as many banks as the West and over five times as many as the South.

The capital stock of these 1,166 banks in the North was $321,905,255, that of the 660 banks in the West $83,906,000, and that of the 220 banks in the South $45,408,985. That is, the banking capital of the North was nearly four times that of the West and about eight times that of the South.

Other banking statistics for 1879 for these three sections of the country were as follows:

	Surplus.	Undivided profits.	Loans and discounts.	Individual deposits.
North	$58,182,821	$31,911,066	$749,322,642	$611,910.657
West	22,324,238	9,348,454	191,506,660	179,278,252
South	8,999,309	3,727,211	85,280,309	64,730,849

The North had about four times as much surplus as the West and ten times as much as the South. Of undivided profits the North had over three times as much as the West and over eight times as much as the South. Loans and discounts in the North were nearly seven times those in the West and nearly nine times those in the South. Individual deposits in the North were four times those in the West and over nine times those in the South.

Thus, when a statement of the condition of the national banks was called for on October 2, 1879, the banks in the North had loans and discounts out to the amount of $749,322,642, while the capital stock, surplus, individual profits and individual deposits aggregated $1,053,- 909,799. The Western banks had $191,506,669 loans and discounts as resources and $294,856,944 of capital stock, surplus, undivided profits and individual deposits. In the South these aggregated liabilities were $123,055,099, with loan and discount resources of $85,280,309. The average deposits per bank in the North was about $525,000, in the West $272,000 and in the South $294,000.

How do these figures compare with the statement of the national banks in 1889? On July 12, 1889, there were 3,230 banks in the country, with an aggregate capital stock of $600,851,640, an increase of 1,182 banks and of nearly $150,000,000 in capital stock. The increase in the number of banks since 1879 had been about thirteen per cent. in the North, eighty-one per cent. in the West and one hundred and thirteen per cent. in the South, while the increase in capital stock was nearly four per cent. in the North, ninety-five per cent. in the West and seventy per cent. in the South.

Other figures for 1889 were as follows:

	Surplus.	Undivided profits.	Loans and discounts.	Individual deposits.
North	$127,582,805	$45,549,875	$1,061,812,372	$852,424 774
West	40,338,597	14,765,698	450,318,506	370,910,925
South.........	21,937,991	7,136,579	179,787,377	139,093,232

It will thus be seen that there was an increase of surplus of forty-five per cent. in the North, eighty-two per cent. in the West and one hundred and forty-six per cent. in the South; of undivided profits an increase of forty-three per cent. in the North, fifty-eight per cent. in the West and ninety-two per cent. in the South; of loans and discounts, forty-one per cent. in the North, one hundred and thirty-six per cent in the West and of one hundred and ten per cent. in the South; and of individual deposits, thirty-nine per cent. in the north, one hundred and seven per cent. in the West and one hundred and sixteen per cent. in the South. In 1879 the percentage of surplus in the North to the capital stock was twenty-seven per cent. and in 1889 thirty-eight per cent. In the West this percentage was about twenty-four per cent. in 1879 and the same in 1889, while in the South the percentage of surplus to capital stock was seventeen per cent. in 1879 and twenty-seven per cent. in 1889.

THE UNLIMITED POSSIBILITIES OF DEVELOPMENT IN THE SOUTH.

The industrial advancement of the South during the last few years has been so rapid that many people, who have failed to appreciate the magnitude of the natural resources on which this progress is based, wrongly imagine that this development must in a few years reach its limit. They cannot comprehend, because they have not studied the subject, that the South's growth can go on indefinitely and yet the limit be not reached.

This point can probably be best illustrated by taking one State, Alabama for instance, as a type of the South and comparing it with Pennsylvania, the typical wealthy State of the North, combining enormous industrial and agricultural prosperity. If it can be shown that Alabama in itself has greater possibilities than Pennsylvania, and is destined in time to surpass the latter in industrial and agricultural wealth, it will be readily admitted that the former has as yet scarcely laid the foundation of its industrial structure. This can be better understood when it is remembered that in 1880 the value of the manufactured products of Pennsylvania was $744,818,445, or nearly $300,000,000 greater than the combined values of the manufactured products of the entire fourteen Southern States in that year, and 57 times greater than the value of Alabama's manufactured products in the same year; in other words, against Pennsylvania's $744,000,000, Alabama had less than $14,000,000 as the value of her manufactured products in 1880. The assessed value of personal property and real estate in Pennsylvania in 1880 was $1,683,450,016, against $122,863,228 in Alabama. In 1880 Alabama had a population of 1,262,344, while Pennsylvania had 4,282,891 ; Alabama had 2,070 manufacturing establishments and Pennsylvania 31,225; Alabama had only four towns or cities having a population of over 4,000, while Pennsylvania had fifty-six.

These statistics show what great progress Alabama must make before it attains even unto Pennsylvania's wealth and population in 1880. To do this it must nearly quadruple its population; increase the capital invested in manufactures from $9,600,000 in 1880 to Pennsylvania's $475,000,000 ; the value of the products of its factories from $14,000,000 to $744,800,000 ; the value of its assessable property from $122,000,000 to $1,680,000,000 ; the number of its factories from 2,000 to 31,000, and its present railroad mileage from 3,000 miles to Pennsylvania's 7,445 miles.

Doubtless many will say that all this is impossible and that Alabama can never reach Pennsylvania's material greatness. This is not, however, to show that Alabama will overtake and surpass Pennsylvania, for the latter State is still pressing forward in development, though even this may be done, but is simply designed to show what immense strides Alabama must make for years to come even to reach where Pennsylvania stood in 1880.

Can this be done? Undoubtedly. If this answer is correct then there need be no fear that Alabama (and Alabama is here used as a type of the whole South) will develop too rapidly or that the limit of its healthy progress will be reached for many generations.

Now if Alabama has greater advantages and resources of minerals, timber, soil, climate, watercourses, &c., than Pennsylvania, and if all these can be utilized to better advantage, and its minerals more easily and cheaply developed, then there is no reason why Alabama should not become as populous and as wealthy as Pennsylvania. The total area (land surface) of Alabama is 51,540 square miles, and of Pennsylvania 44,985 square miles, or a difference of 6,600 square miles in favor of the former. The timber resources of Alabama are immense. In 1880 there were 21,192,000,000 feet of standing pine, while Pennsylvania had only 1,800,000,000, or not one-tenth as much as the former State. Of Pennsylvania's timber interests the census report says: "Merchantable pine has now almost disappeared from the State and the forests of hardwood have been either replaced by a second growth or have been so generally culled of their best trees that comparatively little valuable hardwood now remains. * * * From all parts of the State manufacturers using hardwood report great deterioration and scarcity of material, and Pennsylvania must soon lose, with its rapidly disappearing forests, its position as one of the great lumber producing States."

On the contrary, Alabama, in addition to its immense pine forests, is reported as having much of its territory covered with a rich and varied forest growth of broad-leaved trees, in which oaks, hickories, ashes, walnuts and cherries abound, while there are also great regions covered with heavy forests of cypress, a very valuable timber. Alabama has the material for more than duplicating Pennsylvania's 2,800 lumber mills, with their $21,400,000 of capital, and this will be done as the demand for lumber and woodwork generally increases.

Alabama has nearly 9,000 square miles of coal area, or nearly as much as the entire coal area of Great Britain, and but slightly less than Pennsylvania's. Its iron ore mines are absolutely inexhaustible, according to all human calculations.

Col. A. K. McClure, of Philadelphia, one of the leading men of the times, and who could not be expected to praise Alabama at the expense of his own State, was so impressed several years ago, after a careful study of the subject, with the magnitude of Alabama's mineral wealth and the cheapness of its development that he wrote a most interesting article, from which the following extract is ' taken, and while old to many of the regular readers of the *Manufacturer's Record*, will be new to some who read this issue:

"I have studied the resources and opportunities of the State with special interest, because they are certain to revolutionize some of our chief sources of wealth in Pennsylvania, and the more they are studied the more clear it must become to every intelligent mind that England is not to-day more the rival of the Keystone State in the future production of iron and coal than is Alabama. There is not a source of mineral wealth in Pennsylvania, excepting only our oil product, that is not found in Alabama in equal or greater abundance, with the matchless advantages of climate, of easier and cheaper production, and of vastly cheaper transportation. Nature's great gifts to Pennsylvania have been not only liberally supplemented in Alabama, but to them have been added every possible natural advantage for their cheap development and delivery to the markets of the world. If half the capital and business direction that have been given to make Pennsylvania peerless in the production of mineral wealth had been given to Alabama, her productive wealth would be as great as that of the Iron State, and her population would be nearer five millions than the million and a quarter now scattered over the boundless but almost untouched riches of this sunny commonwealth."

Col. McClure very truthfully says that Alabama is the equal of Pennsylvania in forest, field and mine, and superior in climate, natural highways and cheapness of product. There is, therefore, no reason why Alabama should not surpass Pennsylvania in wealth and population. Our readers can form some idea of how long it will require to do this even at the rate of progress that it is now making.

Alabama—and the South—can grow for generations as rapidly as they are now doing, and still the great development will not be overdone. In this illustration Alabama is contrasted with Pennsylvania, because Alabama has taken the lead in the production of iron and coal in the South, but Alabama is in no way superior in resources or in the possibilities of development to several other Southern States. Tennessee is doubtless fully the peer of Alabama in coal, iron and timber; Kentucky in coal, timber and agricultural resources; North Carolina in iron and timber, and Virginia in combined advantages of soil, minerals and timber. But these States all have enough, and to spare, and it is unnecessary to point out the particular advantages of each one. The South has such a peculiar combination of advantages—coal, iron, timber, cotton, climate, healthfulness, &c.—a combination which exists nowhere else in the world, that it can more than duplicate the coal and iron interests of Pennsylvania, the wood-working interests of the Northwest, and the ' cotton manufacturing of New England.

A GENERAL SUMMARY.

In all other branches of manufacture the South has made equally as great progress as in the few leading ones, the statistics of the growth of which have been given. From a comparatively small business the manufacture of cotton-seed oil has become one of the most flourishing in the South, representing a cash investment of fully $20,000,000, though the nominal capital is greatly in excess of that. In 1880 the South had forty cotton-seed oil mills, with a capital of $3,504,500; there are now 213 mills and over $20,000,000 are invested in the business. The lumber industry in all its branches, from the small saw mill costing a few hundred dollars to the costly furniture factory, has grown probably more rapidly than any other line of manufacturing in the South. It is estimated by conservative authorities that upwards of $100,000,000 have been invested in the purchase of Southern timber lands and the building of woodworking enterprises since 1880, but this is probably much too small a sum, for the sales of timber lands to Northern and Western capitalists run well up into the millions of acres every year.

The mining of phosphate rock has more than doubled. and the manufacture of fertilizers has now become a leading industry throughout the South, especially in connection with cotton-seed oil mills. Thus many millions of dollars which formerly went North for fertilizers are kept at home. Recent discoveries in Florida have shown that that State has the greatest phosphate beds known in the world. Within a few months several million dollars have been invested in the purchase of phosphate lands, and arrangements are being made to mine and ship the rock on a very extensive scale. It is believed, by those who have carefully investigated the magnitude of these phosphate fields, that they will prove of incalculable value not only to Florida but to the whole South. While many millions of dollars will be invested in working them, furnishing employment to a large number of men, the greatest benefits will result through the cheapening of fertilizers to all Southern farmers. This means larger crops produced at a lower cost, and a general improvement of the entire agricultural interests. As the development of the iron mines of the South has permanently lowered the cost of producing iron in this country, thus benefiting the whole conntry, it is probable that the discovery of these Florida phosphates will materially reduce the cost of fertilizers for the entire country.

Within the last few years the growth of the early fruit and trucking business has been one of the most noticeable features of Southern progress. Day after day during the season ocean steamers and full trains of cars, freighted with vegetables and fruit, leave the leading Southern ports for Northern cities. It is estimated that this business now aggregates at least $50,000,000 a year, and it is rapidly expanding. With the increase in population and wealth of the country the demand for Southern fruits and vegetables steadily grows, and they are no longer classed as luxuries, as a few years ago, but are now regarded as necessities of life. This industry and the lumber business, which has assumed great magnitude in eastern Carolina, in Florida, in South Georgia and in Mississippi, are making these sections almost as prosperous and full of life and activity as the mineral regions of the Piedmont and mountain sections of the South.

Everywhere and in all lines the South is at work. Its people are imbued with a spirit of energy and enterprise never surpassed; its vast resources are being opened up and their development is adding to the prosperity of every part of this section, and its manifold attractions and advantages are bringing a steady stream of wealth and of men of enterprise to this fair land. What the South has accomplished in the way of new industrial enterprises may be seen from the following summary of the number organized during four years from January 1, 1886, to December 31, 1889 :

Iron furnace companies	126
Machine shops and foundries	441
Agricultural implement factories	63
Flour Mills	535
Cotton Mills	267
Furniture factories	220
Gas works	101
Water works	331
Carriage and wagon factories	178
Electric-light companies	475
Mining and quarrying enterprises	1,801
Lumber mills, including saw & planing mills, sash & door factories, stave factories, &c.	3,036
Ice factories	293
Canning factories	425
Stove foundries	25
Brick works	565
Miscellaneous iron and steel works, rolling mills, pipe works, &c.	184
Cotton compresses	114
Cotton-seed oil mills	148
Miscellaneous enterprises not included in foregoing	4,415
Total	13,744

It may be well to sum up only a few leading points in the South's growth during the last few years, as given in the preceding pages, and thus convey some general idea of what has been done in that brief period.

In four years nearly 14,000 new manufacturing and mining enterprises have been organized in the South and thousands of old plants greatly enlarged. The list of new enterprises extends over almost the whole range of human industry, embracing pig iron furnaces, foundries, machine shops, steel works, cotton and woolen mills, cotton-seed oil mills, cotton compresses, fruit canning factories, carriage and wagon factories, agricultural implement factories, flour mills, grist mills, saw mills, planing mills, sash, door and blind factories, shuttle factories, handle and spoke factories, barrel factories, shingle mills, furniture factories, tobacco factories, brick-yards, ice factories, fertilizer factories, stove foundries, wire fence factories, lime works, soap factories, tanneries, glass works, gas works, distilleries, potteries, electric-light works, marble and slate quarrying companies and companies to mine coal, iron ore, gold, silver, mica, natural gas, oils, &c.

The number of national banks has increased from 220, with a capital of $45,408,985, in 1879 to 472, with a capital of $76,454,510, in 1889, a more rapid percentage of gain than is shown by the rest of the country.

The railroad mileage of the South has been increased by the addition of nearly 20,000 miles since 1880. Since that year over $800,000,000 have been spent in the building of new roads and improving old ones. The assessed value of property has increased over $1,300,000,000. This does not show the full increase in the value of property, since there is a very large amount of manufacturing property created since 1880 which does not appear in the tax assessments, being exempt by law from taxation. The increase in the true value of property was over $3,000,000,000. In 1880 the South made 397,301 tons of pig iron ; in 1888, 1,132,858, and in 1889 the output was 1,566,702 tons.

In 1880, 6,048,571 tons of coal were mined in the South, and in 1889 the output was over 19,400,000 tons. Cotton mills have increased from 161, with 14,323 looms and 667,854 spindles, in 1880 to 355 mills, with 45,001 looms and 2,035,268 spindles, while many new mills are under constructon and many old ones being enlarged. In 1880 there were 40 cotton-seed oil mills in the South, having a capital of $3,500,000 ; now there are 213, with over $20,000,000 invested.

The value of the South's agricultural products for 1889 was about $850,000,000, against $571,000,000 in 1879. The value of the South's live stock on January 1, 1889, was $569,000,000 while in 1880 it was $391,400,000.

The production of grain rose from 431,074,630 bushels in 1880 to 652,291,-000 bushels in 1889, an increase of over 220,000,000 bushels.

In every line of industry the same tremendous strides of progress are being made.

Presenting these comparisons in tabular form we have the following :

	1880.	1889.
Assessed value of property............	$2,913,436,095	$4,220,166,400
Railroad mileage..............	20,612	40,521
Cost of railroads.....................	$679,000,000	$1,500,000,000
Yield of cotton, bales............. ...	5,755,359	† 7,250,000
Yield of grain, bushels................	431,074,630	652,291,000
Number of farm animals	28,754,243	45,592,536
Value of live stock......	$391,412,254	$569,161,550
Value of chief agricultural products.	$571,098,454	$850,000,000
Coal mined, tons.....................	6,049,471	19,497,418
Pig iron produced, tons.	397,301	1,566,702
Phosphate rock mined.......	190,000	507,708
Number of cotton mills...............	161	355
Number of spindles..	667,854	2,035 268
Number of looms.....................	14,323	45,000
Number of cotton-seed oil mills.......	40	213
Capital invested in cotton-seed oil mills	$3,504,000	$20,000,000
Number of national banks.....	220 ·	472
Capital of national banks.............	$45,597,730	$76,454,510

†Estimated.

SOUTHERN MEN HAVE LED IN THE SOUTH'S DEVELOPMENT.

The statement of Mr. Frederic Taylor, of New York, already quoted, to the effect that the industrial advance of the South has thus far been mainly through the work of Southern people is undoubtedly true. With all due credit to the Northern men who have been active in the development of the South's resources, candor will compel any honest investigator to admit that Southern energy and enterprise mainly are entitled to the credit for what has been accomplished. Southern men led the way. Out of the darkness that developed this section until 1876, they blazed the path to prosperity. They built cotton mills and iron furnaces, and demonstrated the profitableness of these enterprises. Southern men founded and built up Birmingham, which first opened the eyes of the world to the marvelous possibilities of this section. When they had done this, then Northern capitalists seeing the opportunities for money making turned their attention South.

The people of the South do not lack in energy or enterprise. Since the formation of this government they have demonstrated in every line of action—in political life, on the battle field, in literature, in science and in great commercial undertakings—that in any sphere of life they are the

peers of the most progressive men of the world. The masses of the
South have lacked opportunity; to that alone is due their seeming want
of energy. The condition of the country prior to the war and for ten or
fifteen years after its close made agriculture and the professions almost
the only occupations for employment. The former could at the best yield
but poor returns where there was no possibility of diversified agriculture
in its widest sense. With no consumers for diversified farm products it
would have been a waste of time to raise them. Cotton, and cotton
alone, was the only crop for which a market could always be found.

The Northern farmer is enterprising. He raises fruits and vegetables
and engages in dairying and kindred enterprises because he has a home
market for these things. The Southern farmer had none and could not
create one. He might deplore his enforced idleness when he saw his
family in want, but that would not bring him buyers for his eggs or
chickens or fruit when there was no one in his section to consume them.
The almost unlimited amount of work for the mechanics and day laborers
generally at the North enabled every man to find something to do. In
the South there was almost an entire absence of work of this character.
Men hung around the village stores because there was no work to be had
which would yield them any returns. With the development of manufactures there came a great change. The opportunity for work had come,
and the way in which the people who had hitherto been idlers rushed to
the factories, the furnaces and wherever employment could be secured
demonstrated that they only needed the chance to prove their energy.

No sadder sight was ever seen than that of the tens and hundreds of
thousands of Southern people, men and women, suffering in the deepest
poverty which followed the war, and yet forced by circumstances beyond
their power to change, to remain in idleness. It was enough to crush the
life out of them. The greatest blessing that industrial activity has
brought to the South is that it is daily creating new work for thousands
of hitherto idle hands, and creating a home market wherever a furnace
or a factory is started for all the diversified products of the farm. The
latent energy of the people has been stimulated into activity, and the
whole South is at work.

CORROBORATIVE TESTIMONY AS TO THE SOUTH'S DEVELOPMENT BY LEADING PUBLIC MEN.

When the Special Bankers' Edition of the *Manufacturers' Record* was sent out in December, copies were mailed to the President of the United States, to the several members of the cabinet, and to many Senators and Representatives. In every case the paper was accompanied by a letter of advice that it had been sent, and an intimation to the recipient that if willing to give public expression to his views upon the future of the South, or upon the progress made since 1880, as set forth in that publication, a letter to that effect would be appreciated. Many letters of response were received, and with a view to showing how fully the South's progress is appreciated by leading public men, some of these letters are published. These letters are strong endorsements of the remarkable advancement of the South, and of the work of the *Manufacturers' Record* in making known to the world the wonderful resources of that favored land.

EXECUTIVE MANSION,
WASHINGTON, D. C., December 20, 1889.

Editor Manufacturers' Record:

Dear Sir—Allow me to acknowledge the receipt of your favor of the 19th inst., and to express to you the President's thanks for your friendly courtesy in sending to him the copy of the *Manufacturers' Record* containing the article on "The South's Redemption."

Very truly yours,

E. W. Halford

Private Secretary.

VICE-PRESIDENT'S CHAMBER,
WASHINGTON, January 10, 1890.

Editor Manufacturers' Record:

Dear Sir—The rapid development of the South in all lines of commercial enterprise, as shown by the record of the last decade, proves that it is not solely an agricultural section, but the home of a great diversity of industries. This fact brings the South in line with all sections of the country, and the result is sure to be mutually beneficial. I have read with pleasure recent statements in the *Manufacturers' Record* bearing upon the renewed prosperity and rapid development of new enterprises in the South.   Yours very truly,

Levi P. Morton

DEPARTMENT OF STATE,
WASHINGTON, January 11, 1890.

Editor Manufacturers' Record:

Dear Sir—You could not be engaged in a more patriotic work than in making known to the world the rich and varied resources of the Southern States of the Union. Believing that you are promoting this end in the *Manufacturers' Record*, I heartily wish you success in extending the circulation of your valuable magazine.

Very respectfully,

James G. Blaine

TREASURY DEPARTMENT,
WASHINGTON, January 2, 1890.

Editor Manufacturers' Record:

My Dear Sir—My attention has recently been called to the *Manufacturers' Record*, which seems to be especially devoted to the industries of the South, and I have taken much pleasure in looking over the last few issues of this journal. On almost every page there is to be found evidence of the progress of material affairs which has been made in that section, and indications are plentiful of still greater development of those resources which go far towards making a people prosperous and contented. This remarkable growth in the commercial and industrial life of the Southern States is exceedingly gratifying, and is a splendid illustration of the beneficent results of the American principle of protection which has stood guard against the menacing and destructive influences of the old world, while factories and mines are being successfully operated in the new. That the efforts of your paper may do much to aid in the good work at the South I have no doubt, and you have my best wishes for abundant success.

Very truly yours,

W. Windom

POSTOFFICE DEPARTMENT,
OFFICE OF POSTMASTER-GENERAL,
WASHINGTON, D. C., January 11, 1890.

Editor Manufacturers' Record:

My Dear Sir—The industrial advancement of the South, as shown in the pages of the Special Bankers' Edition of the *Manufacturers' Record*, which you have been good enough to send me, is indeed marvelous. The hope of any country, or of any part of any country, is in the honest industry of its people. If to this quality can be added the courageous enterprise which plans and carries forward, and the liberal thrift which spends as well as saves, there can be no question, I should think, of the complete prosperity of the Southern States of the Union to which Northern sentiment and good fellowship, as well as Northern capital, are more and more reaching out.

With great respect, dear sir,

Yours most truly,

Jno. Wanamaker

DEPARTMENT OF THE INTERIOR,
WASHINGTON, January 13, 1890.

Editor Manufacturers' Record:

Sir—In reading your valuable journal my attention has been called to the vast growth of all the material interests of the South, and this department contains within it much that is benefited by this advancement. Your journal commends itself as one of national importance, giving much information affecting public interests not otherwise obtainable.

In the last annual report of this department attention was called to the great advance in the educational interests. It appears from the statistics of the public schools for the decade 1876-77 to 1886-87 that the growth of the public school system, considering the whole country, outstripped the growth of the population. The excess of this increase of enrollment over the increase in population 6 to 14 years of age was 2.1 per cent., and was due to the progress of the public schools, particularly in the South Central Division. The increase there of enrollment (83.4 per cent.) shows an increase over the increase of population (36.8 per cent.) of 46.6 per cent. Much more was said in the report tending to support the general proposition here made.

The exhibitions made in your journal connected with this advance in education and intelligence give assurance of an early and rapid development of all the great resources of the South. It would take more time than I now have at command to speak in detail of the great landed interests this department has under its control, and which are rapidly being disposed of in the Southern States; but the constant and continuous increase in the demand for homes under the general laws of the United States is a cheering indication of the future of that portion of our common country. With intelligence, industry and the resources for development there found, the greatest assurance may be felt that the career on which the "New South" has entered will be maintained and perpetuated if justice is administered to all alike, and the right of each man to his own preserved. These are the foundations at last of all prosperity, and I am confident in the hope that they will not fail the Southern people.

With the best wishes for the success of your paper and the advancement of all the interests that you advocate.

Yours most respectfully,

John W. Noble.

DEPARTMENT OF AGRICULTURE,
OFFICE OF THE SECRETARY,
WASHINGTON, D. C., December 30, 1889.

Editor Manufacturers' Record:

Dear Sir—I am in receipt of your valued favor of the 20th inst., together with the special copy of the *Manufacturers' Record*, containing a most interesting review of the industrial, railroad and financial progress of the South during the last ten years. I am greatly obliged to you for this copy of your valuable paper, and I have read the review which furnishes such remarkable testimony as to the future development of the South with the closest attention and no less gratification.

To refer with any approach to detail to the varied industrial topics covered by the review would be quite impossible within the limits of an ordinary letter. I will merely say a word then on that subject which is naturally of the greatest personal interest to myself—agriculture. In this department of your great industrial development it is especially gratifying to observe the effort on the part of the Southern farmers to diversify their products. The supremacy which the South possesses in the markets of the world as a cotton-producing country there seems little reason to suppose it will ever forfeit, and yet, in this age of wonderful industrial development, it is well for those who think that they stand to beware lest they fall, and self-interest as well as public weal enjoins that we should ever seek to attain the highest standard in everything that we produce. The natural facilities of the South for the production of this great cotton crop, aided and directed by the intelligence which constantly seeks improvement, must assure for all time the supremacy of our Southern States as the cotton-producing region of the world. The South has a climate and a soil well adapted to producing all the crops necessary to provide its inhabitants with food, and the rapid increase in its production of cereals during the past few years is extremely gratifying, and so, also, is the wonderful increase in value of live stock ; and in this connection I would call your attention to the special importance of the horse, dairy and sheep interests. The great development of your manufacturing interests in the South will soon create an extraordinary demand for heavy draft horses. There is no reason why this demand should not be supplied by Southern farmers if they will prepare for it in time. In the dairy interests many sections of the South have already given evidence of most gratifying progress, and I can only say that with the early establishment in this department of a division devoted especially to the dairy, it will be my pleasure, as well as my duty, to aid this development to the fullest extent possible. With reference to the sheep, I notice in this branch of live stock, and in this alone, a falling off in values between 1879 and 1889. I trust that the forthcoming decade will show a very different record, and that, in the meantime, Southern farmers will give more attention than heretofore to the raising of mutton sheep, for which, I am satisfied, a great many sections of the South are peculiarly well adapted.

The subject is almost an inexhaustible one, but to say one-half of what I would like to say in regard to the magnificent field which the South affords to American intelligence and American energy would quite transcend the limits of a letter. I will conclude, therefore, by expressing once more my profound gratification at the magnificent showing made by your interesting review, and congratulating you upon the admirable manner in which you have arrayed these startling facts and figures for the information of the American public.

I remain, very truly yours,

J. M. Rusk

Secretary.

UNITED STATES SENATE,
WASHINGTON, D. C., December 23, 1889.

Editor Manufacturers' Record:

Dear Sir—Your favor of the 19th inst., together with a copy of the *Manufacturers' Record*, has been received. I have not been unmindful of the industrial growth of the South for several years, and have been accustomed to look at your paper for valuable statistics in relation thereto, and your latest *Manufacturers' Record* furnishes a very exhaustive account of the progress the South has made within the last twenty years. You will please accept my cordial thanks.

Very truly yours,

Austin F. Pike [signature]

UNITED STATES SENATE,
WASHINGTON, D. C., January 10, 1890.

Editor Manufacturers' Record:

Dear Sir—I have looked over with much interest the remarkable statements in the special edition of the *Manufacturers' Record* of December 21, 1889, concerning the growth of the Southern States in the production of pig iron, the manufacture of cotton goods and lumber, the building of railroads and towns, coal mining, grain raising and banking. You are right; in some of these things "the history of many Southern towns in the last five years reads almost like a romance." I am glad to see the *Manufacturers' Record* making this exposition of resources and growth; it will accelerate progress. And I wish more of the capitalists who are exploring what Judge Kelly called "the coming El Dorado of American adventure" would come to a "realizing sense" of the magnitude and extraordinary variety of resources of my native State—North Carolina. I had occasion to give them considerable study in preparation for an address at the State Fair in Raleigh a few years ago. North Carolina's ranges of climates, soils, fauna and flora and minerals are unequaled by those of any other State. That is a broad and strong statement. Put it to the test of a thorough examination.

Hastily yours,

[signature]

UNITED STATES SENATE,

WASHINGTON, D. C., January 10, 1890.

Editor Manufacturers' Record:

Dear Sir—I have read with much satisfaction the information contained in the *Manufacturers' Record* of the rapid advance of the various branches of manufacture in the South. The progress made is almost marvelous, and I trust is but a beginning of a still greater advance in the same direction—a diversity of production in a country formerly almost exclusively agricultural. The success of varied mechanical industries will induce a greater variety of agricultural products, and will bring to the South that which is most wanted there—a home market for home products. I trust this prosperity will tend to settle the race conflict upon a fair basis, for with a diversity of pursuits the negro will become more valuable, more independent and more worthy of the rights and privileges of freedom. The prosperity of one section leads to the prosperity of all, and personally I rejoice in every hopeful sign of prosperity in the South as much as in the North, or in the state of Ohio, in which I live.

Very truly yours,

John Sherman

UNITED STATES SENATE,

WASHINGTON, D. C., December 22, 1889.

Editor Manufacturers' Record:

My Dear Sir—Accept my thanks for a copy of the *Manufacturers' Record* containing information as to the progress of the South, which is exceedingly interesting. There is not in the history of the world a progress so marvelous as that of the Southern people since the war.

I do not mean by this to convey the idea that there has not been in other countries a material progress in certain eras equal to that made by the Southern people during the time I have mentioned; but when we consider the circumstances which have environed the South since the war, the increase of material wealth is without a parallel in the history of nations.

If the charges made by the partisan press of the North be true—that the Southern people are systematically engaged in oppressing the negro, and that they spend their days in scheming for that purpose, and their nights in murder and intimidation—then they are beyond question the most remarkable race of people who have existed upon the face of

the earth. If these charges were true it would follow that the Southern
people are able to violate all the laws which properly govern social and
economic conditions, and at the same time attain a degree of prosperity
which amazes the world.

No intelligent man, not blinded with partisan passion and prejudice,
will believe any such thing. On the other hand, the progress made by
the South is a complete and logical refutation of the miserable slang and
falsehood used by demagogues in the North for political purposes.

It is simply impossible that a people addicted to the practices por-
trayed by the Northern press and re-hashed in the halls of Congress,
could use the oppressed and sullen labor of the negro to bring about the
amazing results contained in the special copy of the *Manufacturers'
Record* which you have been kind enough to send me.

This prosperity has been brought about by the exertions of the
Southern people alone, and if it is to continue in that section it must be
done by the same agencies, unvexed by the interference of the Federal
Government. It seems to me that this phase of the question is far
more interesting than any other.

Very truly, &c.,

G. G. Vest.

UNITED STATES SENATE,

WASHINGTON, D. C., December 27, 1889.

Editor Manufacturers' Record:

Dear Sir—I am obliged for your kindness in sending me a copy of
the *Manufacturers' Record* of December 21. It, like other copies that
have come under my notice, contains varied and most valuable information as to the wonderful industrial progress which is being made in the
Southern States of the Union. If the *Manufacturers' Record* could have
a general circulation through those States it could not fail to do much
good by stimulating enterprise and by pointing out places and business
for investments. It would advise our people of their unlimited sources
of wealth and prosperity, and of how to utilize them.

Very respectfully,

John H. Reagan

HOUSE OF REPRESENTATIVES,

WASHINGTON, D. C., January 4, 1890.

My Dear Sir—Not until quite recently did I find time to read, with that care which its importance demanded, the copy of the *Manufacturers' Record* you were kind enough to send me, containing a review of progress at the South during the last ten years. As a Southern man, deeply interested in the welfare of my section, I beg to thank you for the care with which you have collected, and the judgment with which you have displayed the figures which tell so eloquently what our people are doing, and I am especially glad that you have not failed to show that the development at the South has been principally, up to this point, the work of Southern men, and that Northern capital has now begun to come in, simply because Southern enterprise has shown what our resources are. I wish a million copies of the number you sent me were distributed throughout the North. It would aid vastly in the great work which we have now only fairly commenced. The record your paper will make at the close of 1899 will be, I have no doubt, far more wonderful than that of to-day. The decade upon which we are entering is to demonstrate that England can no longer control the iron markets of the world. Speculation has been busy for some time as to the causes contributing to the recent remarkable rise of iron in Great Britain. The better opinion, it seems to me, is that which holds that England has permanently exhausted her capacity to compete with the fresh fields of enterprise we are now opening up in the South. Though we differ among ourselves about the rates of tariff on foreign goods brought into this country, yet we all agree in being thankful that no tariff laws can prevent us from seeking with our iron the markets of the North and the West. In 1900 we shall be rejoicing that our ancestors provided in the constitution that no duty should be placed on exports, for then we will be exporting iron and steel, probably even to Europe. No law can impede our progress, unless Congress should, by such a stretch of power as in 1867, deprive us of the honest and economical State governments which now insure our peace and prosperity, and this is not to be expected.

Very truly yours,

Hilary A. Herbert

HOUSE OF REPRESENTATIVES, U. S.,

WASHINGTON, D. C., January 17, 1890.

Editor Manufacturers' Record:

Those who have given consideration to the matter of the industrial development in the South during the last ten years, and have pressed their investigation in this direction, have marvelled at the tremendous strides which have been made under the fostering benefits of the principle of "protection to American industries." Alabama has become the third in rank among the iron producing States of the Union, and to-day that one State produces more iron than the entire South did four years ago, the first six months of 1889 production of iron in Alabama being over double that of the first six months of 1888.

The manufacture and sale of cypress shingles in Louïsiana has been phenomenal, and the steadily growing demand for cypress lumber and shingles seems to exceed the rapidly increasing supply. The production of Louisiana's rice has steadily developed from 284,000 sacks in 1877-8 to 619,000 sacks in 1889-90 (up to January 10, 1890), and while the proposition may seem bold—with the present protection continued—Louisiana will be able in a comparatively short time to supply the entire United States with all the sugar and rice consumed in the United States.

By the completion of the Muscle Shoals Canal in the Tennessee river, coal may be floated down stream to the Mississippi river and thence to New Orleans at a price that will, by competition with Alabama coal, force the price of fuel down to such a low figure that New Orleans will surely become not only great commercially, but of great importance as a manufacturing city. In 1880 there were in New Orleans 915 manufacturing establishments, employing 8,404 hands, with a product of $18,809,000. In 1889, year ending August 31, there were 2,998 establishments, employing 24,297 hands, and with a product of $44,923,000. Much of the industrial development in the South has been due to the persistent and successful efforts of the *Manufacturers' Record*, which, by its vigilance and enterprise, has informed, stimulated and encouraged a great many who have become important factors in this wonderful march of industrial progress:

Stimulated by your success and animated by a laudable ambition to lead, I can realize the tremendous influence to-day exerted by your efforts towards continued Southern progress and industrial development. Assuring you of my hearty sympathy in your laudable efforts, I remain,

Very sincerely yours,

H. Dudley Coleman

HOUSE OF REPRESENTATIVES, U. S.,
WASHINGTON, D. C., January 13, 1890.

Editor Manufacturers' Record:

Dear Sir—The *Manufacturers' Record* containing a review of the industrial, railroad and financial progress in the South during the last ten years was duly received and read with the deepest interest—I might almost say enthusiasm. I have always regarded the *Manufacturers' Record* as indispensable to anyone who wishes to form an intelligent idea of the changes which are taking place in the South. Accept my thanks for your kindness, and belive me, Very truly yours,

James Phelan

HOUSE OF REPRESENTATIVES, U. S.,
WASHINGTON, D. C., January 14, 1890.

Editor Manufacturers' Record:

. My Dear Sir—I am greatly interested in the industrial progress of the South, and I have watched it with exceeding interest and care. I never doubted that what has occured would be witnessed by our generation.

From the discovery of the continent until the termination of the war all the accumulated surplus of the South found investment in lands and slaves. The country was so new and the lands so fertile that the inducements to put Southern capital into land and into the labor disciplined by ownership were so great as to prevent it finding any other investment ; and the peculiar form of planting in the cotton and sugar States gave to anyone who engaged in it ample occupation for any gifts he might have.

The emancipation of the negro necessarily changed all this, and required some other investments to be found and some other vocations to be followed. The peculiar climate of the South, which permits those residing within its territory to live at so economical a rate, the exhaustless mineral resources, the enormous lumber interests, the unusual river capacity for transportation, rendered it certain that as soon as the losses of the war were repaired the development there would seem to be marvelous. This will continue.

There was before the war a general impression in the North that the slave labor of the South was a competitor of the skilled labor of the North. There never was a greater mistake. The skilled labor of the North took the raw material furnished by the unskilled labor of the South, and without competition inside of our boundary, turned it into the finished fabric. This was terminated by the war, and the daily increasing skill of the Southern labor will furnish competition to the skilled labor of the North, and perhaps upon conditions which will make it dangerous.

I therefore have never doubted, and do not now doubt, the constant and rapid development of the South in all industrial enterprises, and I think before the termination of this century it will be found that we are only on the threshold of that development.

I am, very truly yours,

HOUSE OF REPRESENTATIVES, U. S.,
WASHINGTON, D. C., December 26, 1889.

Editor Manufacturers' Record:

My Dear Sir—I have not had time to do more than give the paper a cursory inspection, but enough to satisfy me that a great and much and long-needed work is being effectively done by you in behalf of the growing South. The possibilities of the South are incalculable; her progress during the present decade (i. e., since 1880) is a sure guarantee of a development of resources and enhancement of values which will amaze those who have not made note of it, and make her the wonder and envy of those who were wont to traduce and embarass her. The madness and wickedness of political folly may impede for a time the growth of her industries and enterprises, but her prosperous career and ultimate triumph are assured. The hope of such success is based upon facts which cannot be removed or nullified, viz: the presence throughout her borders of a brave, intelligent, self-reliant people, and the possession of resources and an environment fixed and unsurpassed. I am rather too far advanced in life to change my residence and too poor in this world's goods (ready cash particularly) to give material aid to any enterprise there or elsewhere, otherwise, I would be there and with my money; but while I live, either in public or private life, my voice and vote will be given in her behalf and interest, and I will always hail with special delight any agency which is devoted to the advancement and welfare of the South. I know of no agency more potent in that direction than the *Manufacturers' Record.*   Very respectfully yours,

HOUSE OF REPRESENTATIVES, U. S.,

WASHINGTON, D. C., January 17, 1890.

Editor Manufacturers' Record:

Dear Sir—I have been an occasional reader of your journal for some considerable time past. It is one of the useful publications of the day. Its mission in bringing to light the heretofore hidden resources of the South is a grand one. The development of these resources, now in its infancy, presents to the world a two-fold marvel. They exist in marvelous quantities, qualities and varieties. This development under the "American system of a protective tariff" has added another marvel by showing their value and tremendous force in building up and making that section rich.

Tennessee and Pennsylvania are very nearly equal in their respective numbers of square miles as well as in geography, topography and the like. Pennsylvania has coal, iron and some timber. Tennessee has coal, iron, marble, copper, zinc, lead, mica and an abundance of timber already known, with gold in some localities in paying quantities. There is not another spot on the face of the globe containing more natural wealth than Tennessee—notably the eastern portion of the State. Take Knoxville, in East Tennessee, as a center, and draw a circle of one hundred and fifty miles every way all around it, thus making the circle three hundred miles in diameter, and Knoxville will stand in that center surrounded by a section containing more natural elements of wealth than are to be found in any other part of the known world. No such natural elements of wealth are to be found in Pennsylvania, and yet the manufacturing industries, the iron, coal and development of that State, and the story of her wealth have been told and retold in every civilized community, while Tennessee, with greater resources in quantity, variety and quality, has been unheard of as a manufacturing State until quite recently. And why? Because the one State had taken advantage of the American policy of a protective tariff and engaged in manufacturing, and thus secured other developments, which follow wherever manufactures are established. The resources of Tennessee lay in the earth and on the earth until such journals as the *Manufacturers' Record* unfolded their marvelous existence, and thus attracted capital and inspired enterprise and caused the magic touch of modern development to be applied. To-day Tennessee begins to rival Pennsylvania. If the American policy is maintained, to-morrow she will pass the Keystone State in the progress and the attainment of riches by her people, by reason of the development of her more abundant resources.

I write to commend and not to argue. The mere statement of the facts makes the argument complete. Maintain the protective tariff and thus secure the development of Southern resources, and all the States of the Union will be blessed through the practical operation of the American policy. A protective tariff is an American measure. It is the conception of a free—a great people. I want to thank you for urging the maintenance of the American tariff. It belongs to America, and Americans should see to it that it is not destroyed The half has not been, and cannot be told of what it is doing for the South. The resources of that section are inexhaustible, and as a native to the manor born, I wish to urge you to continue in making the new revelation, so that section may bloom and boom, as it will by more thorough development.

Very respectfully, &c.

D. C. Hauk

House of Representatives, U. S.,
Washington, D. C., January 20, 1890.

Editor Manufacturers' Record:

Dear Sir—Your special edition of the *Manufacturers' Record* of the 21st December last, setting forth the progress of the South in mining and manufacturing enterprises, makes a splendid showing of the great development now going on in the Southern States and will no doubt be of very great interest to that large number of our citizens who have invested or are looking to investments in that portion of our country. The array of facts and figures that you produce will astonish many of our countrymen North and West, and they are certainly a source of gratification and pride to all friends of the South.

I have been very greatly impressed recently by the attention that is being given by mining and moneyed men to the splendid deposits of iron and other minerals found in such abundance through that whole section of South Carolina lying between the North Carolina line and the prosperous city of Spartanburg. A number of thriving towns have grown up along the line of the Charleston, Cincinnati & Chicago and the Charlotte & Atlanta Air Line Railroads, and large investments of capital have been made by enterprising men in the extensive mineral lands of this section which are now being opened up with most encouraging results.

The development in that portion of the State—particularly in the counties of York, Union and Spartanburg—is largely due to the attention that has been drawn to it through the enterprise of the *Manufacturers' Record.* Let me hope that you will continue the good work in which you are engaged with benefit both to yourself and the country.

Most respectfully yours,

[signature]

House of Representatives, U. S.,

Washington, D. C., December 24, 1889.

Editor Manufacturers' Record:

Dear Sir—I have looked through your issue with considerable care, and with very great interest. Your summary of the progress of the Southern States is a very important work. I trust it will be widely distributed throughout the whole country. It is thoroughly calculated to give, in the most practical manner, better information on the condition and sentiment of our Southern States. Judging from my personal knowledge of some of the localities upon which you report, I am prepared to believe that your statements are exceedingly conservative, and that if anything, they underestimate the progress of the Southern localities. Your work is an exceedingly valuable one, and your periodical has steadily attracted my attention as one of very great value to the South, and, indeed, to the whole country. It is, of course, perfectly idle for fanatics and fault-finders to talk to reasonable men, such as the American people are, about their favorite hobbies in the face of such gratifying practical information as you spread before them.

Very truly yours,

[signature] C. R. Breckinridge

NORFOLK & WESTERN RAILROAD COMPANY.

TO THOSE LOOKING FOR

Manufacturing Sites

· IN · THE · SOUTH. ·

————※————

THE MOST DESIRABLE LOCATIONS in the South
for manufacturing wagons, stoves, agricultural implements, furniture, or for foundries, machine shops, rolling
mills, muck bar mills, nail works, glass works, cotton or woolen
mills, and tanneries, are to be found in Virginia along the line
of the Norfolk & Western Railroad, from Norfolk to Bristol,
and upon its branch lines. Hardwood of every variety; pig
iron from the furnaces at Lynchburg (2), Roanoke (2 in operation and 1 now under construction), Pulaski (1), Radford (1 to
be built in 1890), Salem, Graham and Max Meadows (1 at each
point now under construction), Bristol (1 to be built in 1890);
bar iron from the rolling mills at Roanoke and Lynchburg;

coke and semi-bituminous coal from the Pocahontas Flat Top field; superior gas coals from the mines on the Clinch Valley Extension; glass sand from Tazewell county; cotton from the markets of the Southern States, and wool from all the Western and Southwestern States and Territories at advantageous freight rates. Favorable freight rates made upon raw materials to all factories established upon its line, as well as to points in the United States and Territories upon the manufactured articles.

Those seeking new fields for manufacturing establishments should not fail to investigate the wonderful development of iron, coal and coke industries that have been made within the past five years along the line of the Norfolk & Western Railroad and the advantages offered by the State of Virginia in the supply of cheap raw materials; by the Norfolk & Western Railroad in the matter of freight facilities and rates upon raw materials and for reaching home, far distant and foreign markets, and by the cities and towns along its line in the way of advantageous sites at moderate cost. Many of the cities and towns exempt manufacturing establishments from taxation for a series of years. For further information as to freight rates and sources of supply of raw materials apply to A. POPE, General Freight Agent, ROANOKE, VA., or to

CHAS. G. EDDY,

Vice-President, Roanoke, Va.